GAME LOGIC

Level Up and Create Your Own Games
with Science Activities for Kids

Angie Smibert

Illustrated by Lena Chandhok

More technology titles in the **Build It Yourself** series

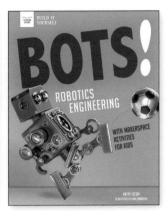

Check out more titles at www.nomadpress.net

Nomad Press
A division of Nomad Communications
10 9 8 7 6 5 4 3 2 1

This book was manufactured by CGB Printers,
North Mankato, Minnesota, United States
June 2019, Job #268931

ISBN Softcover: 978-1-61930-805-3
ISBN Hardcover: 978-1-61930-802-2

Educational Consultant, Marla Conn

Questions regarding the ordering of this book should be addressed to
Nomad Press
2456 Christian St.
White River Junction, VT 05001
www.nomadpress.net

Contents

Interested in Primary Sources?

Look for this icon. Use a smartphone or tablet app to scan the QR code and explore more! Photos are also primary sources because a photograph takes a picture at the moment something happens.

You can find a list of URLs on the Resources page. If the QR code doesn't work, try searching the internet with the Keyword Prompts to find other helpful sources.

🔎 game logic

5000 BCE: . . . . The earliest form of dice are made of sheep knuckles.

3100 BCE: . . . . The game *Senet* is first played.

2650 BCE: . . . . The *Royal Game of Ur* is first played.

1323 BCE: . . . . King Tut is buried with four board games to keep him entertained in the afterlife.

1000 BCE: . . . . *Weiqi (Go)* becomes a popular game.

3000–1000 BCE: . . . . Mancala boards, which include rows of pits, are dug in dirt and carved in stone so people can play.

868 CE: . . . . The first mention of a card game is recorded in China as the "leaf game."

1904: . . . . Lizzie Magie patents the *Landlord's Game,* an early version of the famous and popular game of *Monopoly.*

1968: . . . . Gen Con is founded and about 100 people attend this gaming conference.

1974: . . . . *Dungeons & Dragons* is first published by TSR.

1993: . . . . *Magic: The Gathering* is released by Wizards of the Coast.

TIMELINE

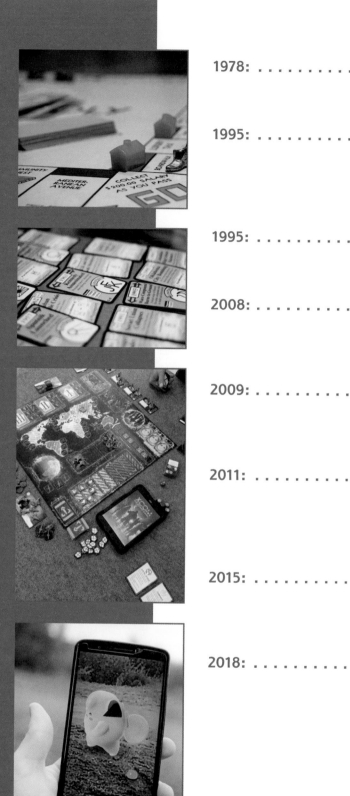

1978: . . . . Spiel des Jahres is founded to reward excellence in game design.

1995: . . . . *Settlers of Catan* is first published in Germany and becomes the first German-style game to gain popularity outside of Europe.

1995: . . . . *Settlers of Catan* wins the Spiel des Jahres.

2008: . . . . *Pandemic*, a cooperative board game, is published and becomes one of the most successful cooperative games.

2009: . . . . Kickstarter is launched, allowing people to raise money to develop games and other creative products.

2011: . . . . *Risk Legacy* is published, a game that changes each time it's played according to the outcome of the last game.

2015: . . . . *Pandemic Legacy* is published, another game in which past outcomes carry over into future games.

2018: . . . . *Azul*, a game based on Portuguese tiles, wins the Spiel des Jahres.

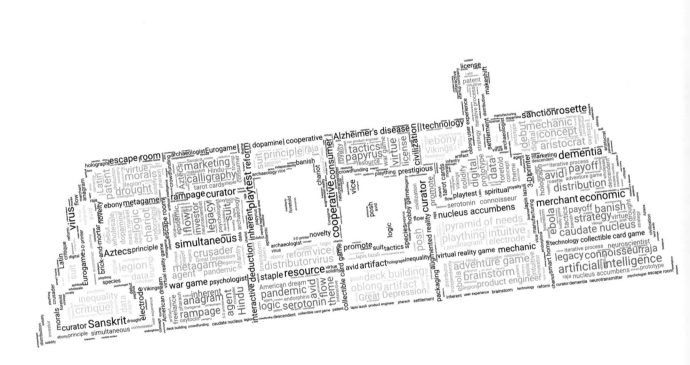

WHAT IS A
GAME?

Games have been around since ancient times. Playing games seems to be a natural part of being human! Whether you love the idea of working together in a cooperative game or the thrill of competing against other players, playing games is a pastime enjoyed on all the continents.

Have you ever wondered how games are invented? Who thinks up the twists and turns of a game of *Clue* or the highs and lows of *Uno*? What's behind the decisions players have to make in *Dungeons & Dragons*? No matter what game it is, a lot of thinking, inventing, and deciding went into it. To get from an idea for a game to a finished product can take years!

Let's take a look at how one game designer made it happen.

ESSENTIAL QUESTION

What is your favorite game to play? Why?

1

WORDS TO KNOW

cooperative: a game that requires players to work together.

user experience: the experience of a person using a product.

pandemic: the outbreak of disease when it spreads across more than one continent. Also the name of a game invented by Matt Leacock.

license: to sell the right to publish to a publisher. The author typically gets royalties, or a percentage of the profits, from sales.

war game: a game based on military experiences.

hobby game: a specialty game played by people who are passionate about it.

avid: eager and enthusiastic.

morals: a person's standards of behavior or beliefs.

tactics: a carefully planned action or strategy to achieve something.

prestigious: something inspiring respect and admiration.

Pandemic Legacy, a game by Matt Leacock and Rob Daviau

credit: mrwynd (CC BY 2.0)

PANDEMIC

Since he was a kid, designer Matt Leacock dreamed of publishing his own board games. He made his own games as a hobby throughout high school and college. After college, he went to work for companies such as AOL and Yahoo, working to improve **user experience** on different technological products. He designed lots of cool things—but he never forgot about games. In fact, he kept designing them on the side.

In 2000, Matt designed a game called *Lunatix Loop*. He printed 200 copies of it on his laser printer and set up a booth at the German game industry show called Spiel. In 2007, Matt pitched the idea for a new game, *Pandemic*, to publishers. *Pandemic* is a cooperative game about fighting outbreaks of disease and **pandemics**. He **licensed** the game to Z-Man Games.

Pandemic has sold millions of copies since it came out in 2009, making it one of the bestselling modern board games. It's also won many design awards and influenced lots of new games. Matt Leacock now designs games for a living!

GAMES AND GOALS

Many tabletop games get their start this way. One or two people have an idea, and they invent a new board or card game.

Take a look at an interview with Matt Leacock at this website.

PS It took Matt lots of tries to become successful!

🔎 Snakes Lattes Matt Leacock

Some inventors are driven by boredom. For example, two bored friends invented *Trivial Pursuit* on a rainy afternoon. Another pair of gamers came up with *Dungeons & Dragons* because they were tired of typical **war games**. And maybe a bored Roman soldier invented tic-tac-toe.

Other inventors want to teach something with their games. The creator of the original version of *Monopoly* wanted to show how greedy landlords could be. The creator of *Life* wanted to teach **morals**! And perhaps an ancient Chinese emperor invented *Go* to teach his son wisdom—or at least military **tactics**.

DID YOU KNOW?

Hobby games are ones designed for **avid** gamers. Hobby games include role-playing games, collectible card games, war games, and some more complicated board games.

The Spiel on Spiel

In 1978, the Internationale Spieltage, or Spiel, opened its doors in Essen, Germany. Spiel is the biggest and most **prestigious** tabletop game trade show in the world. During four days each October, game designers and publishers demonstrate and sell new board games, role-playing games, and card games. More than 150,000 people attend Spiel each year to see what's new in the world of games!

WORDS TO KNOW

plaything: a form of entertainment that people interact and play with. It can be a toy, game, or puzzle.

agent: a player of a game. This can be a person, a computer, or the game itself.

connoisseur: an expert judge in matters of taste.

independently: on one's own or without help.

logic: the principle, based on math, that things should work together in an orderly way.

Most inventors of games, though, just want to create something they love—a great game.

WHAT'S A GAME?

If someone says the word *game* you probably know what they're talking about, right? We know *Scrabble* and kickball are games. We also know a big plastic dinosaur is a toy and a brainteaser is a puzzle.

So, what makes a game different from a toy or a puzzle?

A designer named Chris Crawford (1950–) came up with a helpful way to think about games. Games, toys, and puzzles are all forms of entertainment that we interact or play with. He calls these **playthings**. A toy is something you play with—but without a goal. You're just playing and having fun. Playthings with goals can be puzzles, competitions, or games. We usually work puzzles alone, while competitions and games include many players, called **agents**.

The Spiel des Jahres

In 1978, German game critics started the Spiel des Jahres—or Game of the Year—prize. It's like the Oscars of the board game industry! The prize is given to the best new family-style game. Games are judged on concept, rules, layout, and design. The Spiel des Jahres has recently added separate prizes for children's and **connoisseur** games. Here are some recent winners:

- 2018 *Azul*
- 2017 *Kingdomino*
- 2016 *Codenames*
- 2015 *Push a Monster*

Agents can include human players, the computer, or simply the game itself. In a competition, two or more players compete, but they don't interact with each other to affect the outcome. For instance, running a race is a competition—each person runs their own race **independently**. In a game, however, players either work against each other or they work together against the game.

When game designers develop new games, they have to keep track of many different things. They have to use **logic** to ensure the game makes sense and is fun to play. Otherwise, no one will want to go back to it after playing it only once!

A game is a plaything that players use to interact with each other to achieve a goal. To do that, the players have to follow rules.

In this book, you'll learn about the history, logic, and design of tabletop games. These include board games, cards, dice, and role-playing games. You'll also get the chance to design and play games of your own. You might discover that much more work goes into creating a game than you thought! All you'll need is a little imagination. Let's get started!

data: information, facts, and numbers from tests and experiments.

brainstorm: to think creatively and without judgment, often in a group of people.

prototype: an early version of a design used for testing.

Good Game Developer Practices

Every game developer keeps a notebook to keep track of their ideas and their steps in the game development process. Choose a notebook to use as your own gaming record. As you read through this book and do the activities, keep track of your observations, **data**, and designs by using the following development process. When creating a game, remember that there is no right answer or right way to approach a project. Be creative and have fun!

Concept: What would make a great game?

Design: How will the game work? What will be the goal? Do lots of **brainstorming**!

Implementation: What structure should we give the game? Build a **prototype**!

Testing: Does the game work? How can we improve it?

Evaluate: Analyze your test results. Do you need to make adjustments? Do you need to try a different prototype?

Each chapter of this book begins with an essential question to help guide your exploration of games. Keep the question in your mind as you read the chapter. At the end of each chapter, use your game development notebook to record your thoughts and answers.

ESSENTIAL QUESTION

What is your favorite game to play? Why?

GAME, TOY, OR PUZZLE?

You probably have several board games and card games in your home, as well as puzzles and toys. Crawford called these playthings. Toys are playthings with no goal. Puzzles have goals but players don't interact with each other. Games have goals *and* player interaction. In this activity, you're going to explore what makes a game a game!

❯ Locate several games, puzzles, and toys. Make sure you have at least one of each kind.

❯ In your design notebook, describe each plaything. Is it a game, puzzle, or toy? Why?

❯ Make a chart comparing your games, puzzles, and toys.

Plaything	Goal?	Interactivity?	Toy, puzzle, or game?

Try This!

Pick one of the toys or puzzles. Can you make it into a game? What are the goals and rules of the game? For instance, a Frisbee is really just a toy. But if you add a goal and some player interaction (and rules), you've got a game, maybe Frisbee golf or Ultimate.

GAME RESEARCH

Most game designers are avid players. And they often get ideas for new games from their favorite (or least favorite) games.

❯ **Explore the games you have around the house.** Don't have many? No problem. Some libraries have games you can borrow. You can also download printable versions of many games online at printableboardgames.net.

❯ **Which games are your favorites?** Which are your least favorite? Why?

❯ **Play each game again.** While you're playing, think about what you like and don't like about each game.

❯ **In your design notebook, jot down your favorite parts of each game.** Did you like the theme or a particular rule, for instance? Why are they your favorites?

❯ **What were your least favorite parts?** For instance, do you hate getting eliminated early from a game?

❯ **Start a wish list of themes, rules, and other things you'd like to use in your own game!** And start a list of features you don't want to use.

DID YOU KNOW?

Designer Richard Garfield got the idea for *King of Tokyo* while playing the *Catan Dice Game*. It made him think of *Yahtzee*. So, he mashed up the core of that classic dice-rolling game with Japanese movie monsters!

Try This!

If you like video games, play one of your favorites and make a list of its best and worst features! How are video games different from other games? How are they similar?

MAKE YOUR OWN DICE

Now, we will start making some of our own game pieces! Dice was probably the first game humans invented, and they're often a part of other games. Dice can be made out of many materials, from sheep knuckles to plastic resin. We're going to use paper to make a d6, or 6-sided die.

❯ Draw six 2-inch connected squares in the shape of a cross. Use stiff paper such as heavy construction paper or index cards. You should have four squares down and three across.

❯ Add the numbers 1 through 6 to the center of each square.

❯ Cut out the cross shape.

❯ Fold along the lines until it forms a cube!

❯ Tape the edges together. Tip: Put the same amount of tape on each edge of the dice to make it balanced.

Try This!

Try making a d8 die! Hint: Use triangles rather than squares.

MAKE YOUR OWN DICE GAME!

Most dice games use die or dice with numbered faces. Some, though, have words, letters, symbols, or pictures. For instance, *Boggle* is really a dice game with letters. Let's make a dice game without numbers.

▶ Do a little research on different dice games or games that use dice.

▶ Draw several paper dice (see previous activity). You can make different colored dice, too.

▶ Instead of number, put a simple symbol or picture—such as an emoji—on each face.

▶ Assemble the dice.

▶ Think of a goal and some simple rules for your game. The dice is just a plaything until it has goals, interaction, and rules. For instance, do you need to throw three party hat emojis to win?

▶ Write down the goal and rules in your design notebook.

▶ Play the game with a friend. Is it fun? How might you make it better? Write this in your game development notebook!

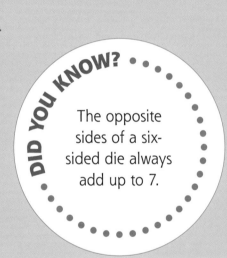

DID YOU KNOW?

The opposite sides of a six-sided die always add up to 7.

Try This!

Make a dice game with words or letters. How does this change the game?

Chapter 1

EVEN PHARAOHS LOVED
BOARD GAMES

Do you like to dive into a round of *Settlers of Catan* in the evening? Do you and your friends start up a game of *Yahtzee* after lunch? Or maybe you prefer a classic game of cards.

Just as you like to play games, so did people who lived long, long ago.

ESSENTIAL QUESTION

Have games changed since we started playing them thousands of years ago?

One way we know this is through **archaeology**. Researchers and scientists have discovered gaming **artifacts** while working on archaeological digs. Some of these games are still being played today.

WORDS TO KNOW

archaeology: the study of ancient people through the objects they left behind.

artifact: an object made by people from past cultures, including tools, pottery, and jewelry.

civilization: a community of people that is advanced in art, science, and government.

BCE: put after a date, BCE stands for Before Common Era and counts down to zero. CE stands for Common Era and counts up from zero. These nonreligious terms correspond to BC and AD. This book was printed in 2019 CE.

pharaoh: a ruler of ancient Egypt.

archaeologist: a scientist who studies ancient peoples through their bones, tools, and other artifacts.

oblong: a stretched-out rectangle with round corners.

ebony: a hard, heavy wood.

papyrus: paper made from the papyrus plant, used by the ancient Egyptians.

The **civilization** of ancient Egypt flourished in North Africa for more than 3,000 years. A man named Tutankhamun (c. 1341–c. 1323 **BCE**) ruled Egypt as **pharaoh** for 10 years, until he died in 1323 BCE.

In 1922, famed **archaeologist** Howard Carter (1874–1939) discovered Tutankhamun's tomb in the Valley of the Kings. When Carter opened the tomb, he unearthed one of the greatest treasures of Egyptian artifacts.

Tutankhamun (also known as King Tut) had been buried with more than 5,000 items, including a solid gold mask and coffin, thrones, precious stones, trumpets, daggers, and four board games. The ancient Egyptians believed in life after death, called the afterlife, and that they needed their belongings in the afterlife—even games!

Dice

Dice was the first tabletop game. In 2013, archaeologists found 49 small carved and painted stones in southeast Turkey, dating to about 3000 BCE (5,000 years ago)! About the same time, other people in the Middle East and Asia made dice using flat sticks, carved knuckle bones, and turtle shells. Later civilizations made dice out of materials, such as glass, metal, ivory, and marble. Ancient dice came in many different shapes. Four-sided, pyramid-shaped dice were found with the *Royal Game of Ur*, which dates back to around 2500 BCE. Archaeologists found cube-shaped dice in China dating to 600 BCE and in Egyptian tombs from 2000 BCE.

SENET (3100 BCE)

One of the board games buried in King Tut's tomb was the game of *Senet*. King Tut had a very ornate set, fitting for a king. The ivory game board had 30 squares, divided into three rows of 10. It sat on top of an **oblong** box with a drawer for the pieces. The box itself sat on cat legs carved out of **ebony**. The paws rested on golden drums.

Though splendid, King Tut's *Senet* board was not the first one archaeologists had found. *Senet* is sometimes called "the game of 30 pieces" and it had been turning up in archaeological digs since the beginning of the nineteenth century. The earliest *Senet* game dates from 3100 BCE. That's when the civilization of ancient Egypt began.

It's amazing to think that a board game saw the rise and fall of a powerful ancient civilization.

Archaeologists also discovered paintings on tomb walls of Egyptians playing the game. One painting even showed players boasting over who would win the game! *Senet* has been found scratched into temple floors as well as drawn on **papyrus** scrolls. And *Senet* is mentioned in the Egyptian *Book of the Dead*. It describes playing *Senet* as one of the occupations of the dead!

Egyptian Queen Nefertiti playing
Senet, circa 1298–1235 BCE

A *Senet* board inscribed for Pharaoh Amenhotep III, circa 1390–1353 BCE

credit: Brooklyn Museum, Charles Edwin Wilbour Fund

Today, the game poses a mystery for us. No one is quite sure how to play it. No instructions have been found. Some modern game makers have tried to come up with their own rules, but we might never know how people in ancient Egypt played the game.

Fortune-Telling Games

Ancient people used many games, such as *Senet*, the *Royal Game of Ur*, and even playing cards, not only for fun but also for **spiritual** purposes. The players might have thought the game **foretold** the future, gave them a peek into the afterlife, or even let them speak to the dead. Some modern players still use **tarot cards** to tell fortunes, too. Why? One reason might be the way our brains work! Human brains are very good at recognizing patterns. This ability helped early humans survive. They could easily pick out a leopard hiding in the trees or tell a poisonous mushroom from one that was safe to eat. Today, we use pattern recognition to find our way home, diagnose disease, and discover new planets. However, humans tend to assign meaning to some patterns—even when there isn't any. So, ancient game players might have seen patterns emerge in a game such as *Senet* or *Ur*—or tarot cards—and then gave them meanings having to do with their futures!

But does this matter? Game experts point out that the rules to games change quite a lot as time passes and new generations pick up the game. Today, you can still find *Senet* board games for sale. An ancient Egyptian would recognize the game board, even if they didn't quite recognize the rules.

Some experts on ancient Egypt think *Senet* was more than just a game.

DID YOU KNOW?

On the walls of Queen Nefertari's tomb (d. 1255 BCE), she's shown playing *Senet* by herself. Perhaps this was a one-person game, like solitaire!

Egyptians may have used *Senet* to learn what lay ahead of them in the afterlife—perhaps they even used the game to contact the dead. The ancient Egyptians believed that their souls would gather on the sun god Ra's barge at sunset. The barge would take them on a journey through the underworld. Along the way, sinners would be punished and destroyed. Those souls who survived the trip would reunite with Ra and live forever. Egyptologist Peter Piccione thinks the markings on later *Senet* boards reflected the soul's journey through the afterlife! The game might have been used to foretell whether the player's soul would make it through the underworld.

ROYAL GAME OF UR (2650 BCE)

Howard Carter also found the *Royal Game of Ur* in King Tut's tomb. Like *Senet*, the *Royal Game of Ur* is much older than Tutankhamun himself. Archaeologists first discovered this game in the Royal Tombs of Ur in what is now southern Iraq.

Founded around 4000 BCE, Ur was one of the richest and largest cities in the ancient world. When it was first built, Ur was a coastal city on the Persian Gulf.

WORDS TO KNOW

drought: a long period of little or no rain.

lapis lazuli: a deep-blue stone.

rosette: a design shaped like a rose.

curator: a person who collects and organizes items in a museum.

merchant: someone who buys and sells goods.

descendent: a person related to someone who lived in the past.

Unfortunately, as time passed, the coastline shifted, moving Ur inland. War, **drought**, and invaders eventually left Ur empty and covered with sand by around 500 BCE.

About the same time Carter was discovering King Tut's tomb, another archaeologist, Leonard Woolley (1880–1960), started excavating Ur. In the city's royal cemetery, Woolley found what became known as the *Royal Game of Ur*, dating from 2650 BCE. This board had belonged to a princess.

The squares on the wooden board were made of shells. Strips of **lapis lazuli**, a brilliant blue gemstone, separated the squares. The dumbbell-shaped board was decorated with eyes, **rosettes**, and geometric patterns. Archaeologists later found versions of the game across the Middle East.

The Royal Game of Ur includes not only the board, but also two sets of markers and four-sided dice. The rules remained a mystery until the 1980s. Irving Finkel (1951–), a **curator** at the British Museum, discovered a forgotten clay tablet.

Checkers

Checkers, or draughts, might have its roots in the *Royal Game of Ur*. Also, the Egyptians played a similar game that dates back to 1400 BCE. These games used pieces on a board. The Egyptian version was so popular it was played for thousands of years. Neither were exactly like checkers, though.

The modern game of checkers was invented around 1100 CE in France. Players used backgammon pieces on a chessboard. Unlike chess, each piece, called a "fers," could move the same way. The game itself was called *Fierges*, or *Ferses*. In the thirteenth century, rules for crowning pieces were added. By the fifteenth century, people were writing books about checkers. The first championship tournament was held in 1847. Today, millions of people still play checkers in their homes, online, or in competitions!

He translated it and found it was a rule book for the *Royal Game of Ur*—it's a race game! Players use dice made from sheep knuckles to move pieces from one side of the board to the other.

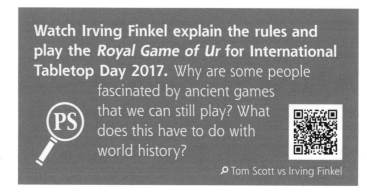

Watch Irving Finkel explain the rules and play the *Royal Game of Ur* for International Tabletop Day 2017. Why are some people fascinated by ancient games that we can still play? What does this have to do with world history?

🔍 Tom Scott vs Irving Finkel

The game was also used to tell players' fortunes. Squares were inscribed with predictions similar to those you might find in fortune cookies, such as "you'll find a friend" or "you'll become powerful like a lion."

Much like the people of Ur, the game died out in the Middle East. However, before it did, a group of Jewish **merchants** took it with them to India. These people settled in Kochi, a city on the southwest coast. After World War II, their **descendants** returned to Israel with a version of the *Royal Game of Ur.*

One of the game boards found by Leonard Woolley in the city of Ur

Latin: the language of ancient Rome and its empire.

chariot: a small cart with two wheels and a platform, pulled by horses.

legion: a large group of soldiers in ancient Rome.

Crusader: a European soldier who took part in one of the wars fought in the Middle East during the eleventh through thirteenth centuries.

BACKGAMMON (2000 BCE)

Have you ever played a game of backgammon? In this game, you roll dice and move multiple pieces along a board in a race to have all your pieces home free before your opponent.

The ancient Romans played two games that were very similar to modern backgammon. The Greeks and Romans imported the older of the two games from the Middle East. This game was known as *ludus duodecim scriptorum*, which in **Latin** means the "game of 12 markings." The Romans made some changes to the game, which they called *tabula* (Latin for "table").

A *ludus duodecim scriptorum* game board from the second century CE
credit: wnhsl (CC BY 2.0)

Both *ludus duodecim scriptorum* and *tabula* were popular, and Romans often played for money. Archaeologists have found game boards carved into the tops of tables in the ruins of Pompeii, a Roman city destroyed by a volcano in 79 CE. There, they've even found a painting of *tabula* players getting kicked out of a tavern!

DID YOU KNOW?

Until recently, historians thought backgammon was the game humans have been playing the longest. When Irving Finkel discovered that the *Royal Game of Ur* was still being played in modern India, he realized that *Ur* was the longest continuously played game in the world.

Emperors loved the game as much as the common folk did. Emperor Claudius (10 BCE–54 CE) even wrote a book about *tabula*. He also had a board installed in his **chariot**!

Both the board and goal of *tabula* were identical to modern backgammon. The game is a mix of skill and luck. The backgammon board has 24 triangular points. With a throw of the dice, each player tries to move their 15 stones, or checker-like pieces, from point to point around the board. The winner is the first to "bear off" or move all their pieces off the board.

Roman **legions** spread *tabula* throughout the Roman Empire. After the empire fell, though, the game began to fade in Europe.

Europeans rediscovered the game after Crusaders brought it back with them from the Middle East, where it was still played.

A tapestry showing people playing *tabula* in the Middle Ages

credit: taken from *Codex Buranus*, a manuscript of poems from the eleventh and twelfth centuries

The game and its variations became very popular in Europe by the seventeenth and eighteenth centuries. By then, a British version of the game had surfaced, called backgammon. The word *backgammon* comes from the English words "back" and "game."

WORDS TO KNOW

solidify: to make something more solid or stronger.

banish: to send someone away from a country or place as an official punishment.

artificial intelligence (AI): the intelligence of a computer, program, or machine.

calligraphy: the art of beautiful writing.

strategy: a careful plan for achieving a goal. Also, the skill of making and carrying out those plans.

A modern backgammon board

DID YOU KNOW?

Backgammon, under its various names, has been played continuously for more than 4,000 years!

In 1743, Edmond Hoyle (1672–1769), a famous card and board game historian, **solidified** the rules of backgammon in a book called *A Short Treatise on the Game of Backgammon*. The rules have remained the same since.

WEIQI, OR GO (1000 BCE)

The ancient Chinese game *Weiqi* (pronounced way-chee), is thought to be about 3,000 years old. Many legends surround its creation, but no one it quite sure how *Weiqi* actually began.

> One legend claims that Emperor Yao (2356–2255 BCE) invented the game to teach his cruel son wisdom.

It didn't work. The son mastered the game, but didn't change his ways. The emperor **banished** his son—and made a farmer the next ruler of China.

AlphaGo

Since the 1950s, **artificial intelligence (AI)** researchers have been trying to program computers to play more and more complex games. The researchers reason that if a computer can beat a human at chess or Go, then they may be one step closer to achieving artificial intelligence. Go is one of the most complex games humans play. In 2015, an AI computer program called *AlphaGo* beat a professional human Go player for the first time. The program defeated three-time European champion, Fan Hui (1981–). *AlphaGo* learned the game by studying thousands of human players, both amateur and professional. *AlphaGo* went on to beat legendary player Lee Sedol (1983–), the next year. In 2017, a new AI, *AlphaGo Zero*, taught itself how to play Go—and arguably became one of the best Go players of all time.

No matter how it came about, *Weiqi* became an important part of Chinese culture. By the Middle Ages, Chinese civil servants were expected to master the game as well as arts such as painting and **calligraphy**.

Today, the game, also called Go, is immensely popular throughout East Asia and is played all over the world.

Go is a **strategy** game. The board has a grid of 19 by 19 squares. The rules are simple. Two players take turns laying down black or white stones on the grid.

The goal is to surround the other player's stones and take them prisoner. To win, a player must capture the most territory and prisoners. The game of *Go* may sound simple, but it requires very carefully planned actions because of the number of moves that are possible.

DID YOU KNOW?

When the game of *Weiqi* spread to Japan around 500 CE, the Japanese changed its name to Go.

After the first two moves in a *Go* game, 130,000 next moves are possible!

CHESS, OR *CHATURANGA* (SIXTH-CENTURY CE)

Many schools and afterschool programs have chess clubs where kids match their strategy skills on the checkered board. Do you play chess? This game has a lot of history behind it!

India's Gupta Empire (c. 320–550 CE) gave us a game called *Chaturanga*. This is the common ancestor of modern forms of chess. *Chaturanga*, or *catur* for short, is a four-player war game. The word *chaturanga* means "four limbs" in **Sanskrit**. Played on a checkered board, *catur* pits military pieces— **infantry**, horsemen, elephants, and ships commanded by a **raja**—of the four players' armies against one another.

Originally, players rolled dice to determine how pieces moved. Later, dice were removed from the game because the **Hindu** Laws of Manu opposed gambling. The game eventually evolved into a two-player game.

When Indian merchants traveled, they took the game with them. The game spread to Persia, and when Muslim armies attacked Persia, the men took the game back to their homes—and changed it yet again. Arab game makers made the shapes more abstract.

As people traveled and traded, they brought the game to Europe. Europeans eagerly adopted the game—and made their own changes. Just as earlier cultures did, Europeans of the Middle Ages added pieces that reflected their lives— knights, bishops, and queens.

By 1300, the rules of chess as we know it today were established. Chess is a game of strategy that requires players to think ahead several moves and develop different plans based on an opponent's actions. How is this similar to a battlefield?

Queens Take Charge of Chess

Early versions of chess could be very slow. As years passed, players in various countries tried different ways to speed up the game. Most didn't stick. In the 1300s, though, European players hit upon the idea of making some pieces more powerful. By the fifteenth and sixteenth centuries, the queen was the most powerful piece on the board. She could move in any direction for as many spaces as she liked on the board. This reflected what real queens were doing at the time—taking charge of countries across Europe. Powerful women ruled in Spain, Italy, and England. Powerful queens changed chess into a more complex and thrilling game.

MANCALA (3000–1000 BCE)

Popular in Africa, the Middle East, and southern Asia, mancala is really a family of approximately 800 games. They all use the same type of board and "sowing" **mechanic** but with different rules. The game board has rows of pits, with a home pit at each end. Players move "seeds" from pit to pit in order to capture the most seeds. Sound simple? It can be tough to master! If you can get the timing right, you can take seeds from your opponent and win the game.

Historians don't agree where mancala was born. Some think mancala originated in Egypt in at least 1400 BCE. Archaeologists have found mancala game boards in Egyptian ruins. Other historians think mancala came from Sumer—the earliest-known civilization, in what is now Iraq. According to historians, Sumerian traders brought the game to Egypt and Africa. Still other historians think mancala started in Africa. How can different historians come to so many different conclusions?

The bottom line is that we don't know whether mancala began in Africa or the Middle East.

DID YOU KNOW?

Mancala comes from the Arabic word, *nagala*, which means "to move."

Nor do we know when the first game was played, only that it was sometime between 3,000 and 5,000 years ago. Why? Often, people may have played a mancala game on a **makeshift** board or even by digging small pits in the ground. And they may have played with actual seeds. All of which make the game hard to trace! We do know, however, that various games moved along trading and slave routes.

Play mancala! Try your skills with the computer as your opponent at this website. Can you learn to count the stones and the spaces to maximize your points?

PS

play mancala

The most widespread and simplest mancala game is called *Oware*. Its board has two rows of six pits. At the beginning of the game, players fill each pit with four seeds. These can be shells, nuts, pebbles, or seeds. Players take turns picking up seeds from one pit on their side of the board and then dropping one seed into each of the next pits until they run out. This is called "sowing." Players capture, or harvest, seeds when only two or three seeds are left in the opponent's pits.

PLAYING CARDS (C. 800 CE)

Playing cards are thought to have originated in China. About 868 CE, a Tang dynasty writer describes Princess Ton Cheng playing the "leaf game." It was a card game! During the following centuries, playing cards spread to India, Persia, and then Egypt. Each culture produced cards with **suits**. In the second half of the fourteenth century, Arabs brought playing cards to Europe.

Playing cards evolved to fit the culture—and technology—of the players. For instance, Arabic suits included cups, swords, coins, and polo sticks. Italian and Spanish card makers adapted these, changing polo sticks to batons. German cards had hearts, acorns, bells, and leaves. Then French and English card makers changed the suits to the hearts, clubs, diamonds, and spades we use today. They also simplified the designs of the suits to make them easier to print.

WORDS TO KNOW

trump: a playing card or suit that's chosen above others to win a trick when a card of a different suit is played.

We've been playing games for at least 5,000 years—and probably longer. Games no doubt predate the written word! Every civilization loved their games. Pharaohs were even buried with them so they could play them in the afterlife. Today, we still play some of those ancient games, along with classics from the last century and exciting new ones from this one. In the next chapter, we'll take a look at some of the games we play today.

Trick-Taking Games

Many card games involve taking a trick. That is, each person plays a card in turn, and the best card takes them all, called a trick. The winner is usually the player or team with the most tricks or points. Trick-taking games include whist, bridge, hearts, and spades.

Whist is a trick-taking game from England. The game has gone through a few names and changes. The earliest game (1500s) was called trump. By the eighteenth century, the game became whist. A four-player game, whist can be played with or without partners. The last card dealt is the **trump** suit. The winner is the first to reach either five (U.K. rules) or seven (U.S. rules) points.

Bridge grew out of whist. By the nineteenth century, the new game was more popular. Like whist, bridge is played by four people. Several types of bridge have been played through the years. Depending on the type of bridge, the trump suit is selected either by the dealer or by players bidding. The winning partners have the most tricks or points at the end of the hand.

Another four-player game, hearts first came to the United States in the 1880s. Hearts has its roots in a much older game called reverse or reversi. The goal is to avoid taking tricks that contain hearts. The winner has the lowest score!

Similar to whist and bridge, spades became popular in the mid-to-late twentieth century. The game is played by four players in partnerships. The trump suit is always spades, but players bid on how many tricks they think they can win.

ESSENTIAL QUESTION

Have games changed since we started playing them thousands of years ago?

RESEARCH AN ANCIENT GAME

Humans have been playing games for thousands of years. The Egyptians played *Senet* and the *Royal Game of Ur*. Romans played backgammon—and versions of tic-tac-toe. The Aztecs played *Patolli*. Why are people still playing games that were invented thousands of years ago?

DID YOU KNOW?

Cards are not used just for playing games. They've been used for fortunetelling, teaching, songs, and baseball.

❯ **Use the internet or head to the library and research one of the ancient games mentioned in this chapter or find a different one on your own.** Pick one that historians know the goals and rules for, such as the *Royal Game of Ur*.

❯ **What did the game look like?** Sketch it in your design notebook.

❯ **How was it played?** Write out the goal and rules. Are they simple or complicated?

❯ **Create the game on paper.** For instance, if you're researching the *Royal Game of Ur*, draw a board on paper, complete with the patterns on the squares.

❯ **Make appropriate game pieces.** For instance, for *Royal Game of Ur*, you might use black and white buttons. If the game needs dice, you can make them out of paper! You can also use pieces from a modern game.

❯ **Play the game with a friend!** Was it fun? Why or why not?

Try This!

Research a game that we don't know the exact rules for—such as *Senet*. Try to come up with your own rules and test them by playing with a friend. How successful are the rules?

WORDS TO KNOW

Aztecs: a Native American people who established an empire in central Mexico between 1300 to the 1500s.

MAKE YOUR OWN CARDS

People have been making playing cards by hand for thousands of years. Some cultures block printed the designs—others hand-painted them. Today, of course, card makers print them on printing presses, and you can even print them yourself on a personal printer. In this activity, you'll be designing your own cards.

> **Research suits and designs used on playing cards for inspiration.** You can find lots of different playing cards online and in books.

> **Come up with an idea for four suits.** Sketch them out in your design book. How will you make them all distinctive yet related?

> **Count out 52 index cards.** You can also cut out 52 cards from heavy construction paper. Divide the cards evenly into four piles, one for each suit.

> **Draw or paint your cards!** For each suit, you need a king, queen, jack, plus cards 1 through 10. Or, you can make up your own royalty cards.

> **Play the cards with a friend.** Are there any flaws in your design? How can you make them better?

DID YOU KNOW?

French card makers in the late sixteenth century originally said the kings in a standard deck of cards represented real historical rulers. The king of spades was David, king of Israel. The king of clubs was Alexander the Great. Charlemagne was the king of hearts, and the king of diamonds was Augustus Caesar, the first Roman emperor.

Try This!

Design your suits using a computer program, such as *Publisher*, and print out your cards. How are these different from your handmade ones? Which do you like better?

BLOCK PRINTING

Card makers in the Tang dynasty in China block printed playing cards. Block printing involves carving a design in a wooden block, inking it, and then pressing the design onto paper. In this activity, you'll design the back of your cards and block print them yourself—using a potato!

❯ **Come up with a simple design or pattern for the back of your cards.** Sketch it in your design notebook. The design should be simple enough for you to carve into the flat surface of a potato.

❯ **With an adult's help, cut a potato in half.** Set one half aside. You can use this for another design.

❯ **Draw your design on the face of the potato.**

❯ **Carefully carve around the design with a paring knife.** The design should be raised a bit. You may need to carve away a little excess potato.

❯ **Make a test print.** Dip the design in the ink and then gently press it on a sheet of paper or a spare index card. Lift the potato. The paper should have your design! You may need to experiment a bit to get your technique down.

❯ **Now you're ready to print the backs of your playing cards.** Repeat the above step for each card and then let them dry.

Try This!

Instead of a potato, use an everyday object—such as the tines of a fork or a bottle cap—to print a design on your cards. Can you still make something original and interesting?

MAKE A MANCALA BOARD

Mancala is a family of games that may have originated in Africa or the Middle East. The games use similar boards, playing pieces, and game play. Most boards have two rows of six pits with two home pits, one on each end. Pits are also called holes, and the home pit is often called the store.

❯ **To make the board, carefully cut the top off an egg carton.** Flip the top over and cut it in half.

❯ **Slide each half underneath the bottom of the carton with 2 to 3 inches of the end exposed.** These form the "home" portions of the board. Glue or tape each home into place.

❯ **Decorate your mancala board.**

❯ **For the playing pieces, you need at least four seeds for each pit, or 48 total.** For some games, you need up to seven per pit.

🔎 how to
play mancala

❯ **Test your mancala game!** You can find instructions for playing mancala at this website.

Try This!

At the beginning of the game, add more seeds to each pit. How does that affect your strategy?

Chapter 2

MODERN GAME
CHANGERS

Ancient games such as mancala, chess, backgammon, and *Go* have endured the tests of time and geography, traveling around the world and still being played by people today. We also play loads of new games invented in the modern era. These games were created for many reasons.

ESSENTIAL QUESTION

Why do people invent new games?

For example, Milton Bradley (1836–1911) and Lizzie Magie (1866–1948) were two people who invented their games to teach. Others designed their games to make money. Still other people designed them just for the fun of it. They were all modern game changers!

WORDS TO KNOW

morality: the distinction between right and wrong or good and bad behavior.

aristocrat: a member of a ruling or wealthy class of people.

virtue: any good quality or trait.

vice: a bad behavior or habit.

American dream: an American ideal that says material prosperity means success.

You might not think games can teach **morality**, but a young man named Milton Bradley decided to invent a game to do just that. That wasn't his first intention when, in 1860, he bought a printing press and opened up his own printing business. Orders poured in—at first. By summer, though, the press sat idle. Milton had no customers.

To cheer him up, Milton's friend invited him to play a board game called *Mansions of Happiness*. Invented in 1800, the game was a dark, religious twist on a much older game called the *Game of the Goose*. It was a simple race game enjoyed by wealthy **aristocrats**, who liked to bet on the outcome of the game. *Mansions of Happiness*, however, was about avoiding sin to achieve happiness. Immediately after playing *Mansions*, Milton decided he wanted to design his own game—and he had the technology to do it. His printing press was idle no more.

And his game was one of the first modern game changers.

The game Milton Bradley designed was called the *Checkered Game of Life*. With it, he wanted to teach morality. Players moved around the board, landing on different **virtues** and **vices**. Virtues included honesty, bravery, and industry, while vices included gambling, idleness, and crime. Virtues could lead a player down the road to happiness, success, and wealth. Vices led to disgrace, poverty, prison, and even death. The first player to reach "Happy Old Age" won. The moral of the game was that everyone could overcome setbacks if they strived for goodness.

Game of the Goose

Game of the Goose was one of the first commercially produced board games. In the sixteenth century, Francesco de Medici (1541–1587) of Italy sent the game to King Felipe II (1527–1598) of Spain. The *Game of the Goose* became one of the most popular games in Europe at the time.

You can see what the original game looked like at this website.

🔍 Museum of Play goose

The game was a hit! Milton Bradley sold 40,000 copies in the first year. Why do you think people wanted to play his game? Were they doing to it try to be better people?

By 1900, the game had become much less popular. Other game makers, such as the Parker Brothers, were making games that were all about having fun. They released games about racing bicycles and exploring the North Pole. The *Checkered Game of Life* faded away, as people chose fun over morality.

But in 1960, the Milton Bradley Company brought the game back as the *Game of Life*. This time, the game focused more on the **American dream**. The game board portrayed life as a long, winding road. Sometimes, the road forked. Players went to college, got a job, and got married. They might become doctors or farmers. In the end, they hoped to retire to Millionaire Acres. Again, the game was a hit. Have you ever played the *Game of Life*?

The *Game of Life* changed with the times—and continued to do so through the next decades.

The *Game of Life* from 1977

reform: a change to improve something.

inequality: differences in opportunity and treatment based on social, ethnic, racial, or economic qualities.

principle: an important idea or belief that guides an individual or community.

patent: a government license that gives an inventor or creator the sole right to make and sell a product or invention.

critique: a judgment that expresses an opinion about something.

MONOPOLY

In the late nineteenth century, the rich were getting richer and the poor were getting poorer. One **reform** movement believed that taxing land—and only land—would help fix this **inequality**. In 1903, Lizzie Magie invented a game she hoped would teach these **principles**. She **patented** the *Landlord's Game* in 1904. In this board game, players snatched up as much land as they could, leaving other players broke. She intended the game as a **critique** of greedy landowners, though in the end, her intentions backfired spectacularly.

Lizzie tried to sell her game to Parker Brothers in 1904, but they rejected it.

They said it was too political. However, other people played the game—and made their own versions of it. One of those versions was called *Monopoly*.

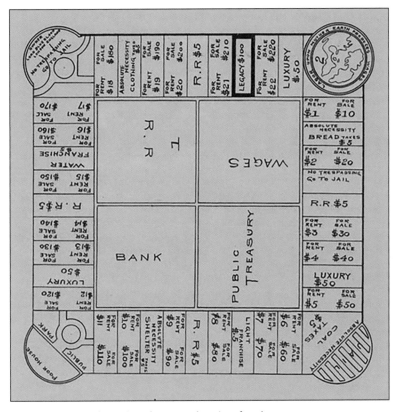

The printed patent drawing for the game board invented by Lizzie Magie

The iconic shoe piece
credit: Rich Brooks (CC BY 2.0)

DID YOU KNOW?

Early *Monopoly* tokens included the lantern, purse, rocking horse, cannon, iron, shoe, and thimble. Today, the only original tokens still in use are the battleship, race car, and top hat.

In 1935, Parker Brothers bought *Monopoly* from a man named Charles Darrow (1889–1967). After they made a few improvements to the game, demand for it started rolling in. When the company tried to patent the game, however, they found out it wasn't Charlies Darrow's game to sell. It was Lizzie Magie's! Parker Brothers privately bought the rights from her. Publicly, the company pretended that Charles was the inventor. By 1936, Parker Brothers had sold 1.75 million *Monopoly* sets.

WORDS TO KNOW

simultaneous: at the same time.

Great Depression: a severe economic downturn during the late 1920s and 1930s that spread around the world.

economic: having to do with the resources and wealth of a country.

anagram: a word or phrase made by changing the order of the letters in another word or phrase.

DID YOU KNOW?

On August 27, 2008, 3,361 players united to break the Guinness World Record for "world's largest **simultaneous** game of *Monopoly*."

By 2008, more than 250 million sets of *Monopoly* had been sold. It is one of the most popular board games in history. Hasbro, the company that now owns the game, produces dozens of versions, including *Star Wars* and *Gamer Monopoly*. Have you played different versions of *Monopoly*?

SCRABBLE

Local *Monopoly*

Hasbro makes dozens of variations of *Monopoly*, including *Star Wars*. In addition, thousands of *Monopoly* versions exist! Most are almost exact copies of the original—with just the places renamed for a particular city or school. For instance, Dublin in Ireland, Aspen in Colorado, and Indiana University all have their own *Monopoly* editions. Some companies have also made *Monopoly* editions based on sports, such as football and hockey, as well as on particular teams.

In 1931, a man named Alfred Butts (1899–1993) lost his job. It was the middle of the **Great Depression**, and many millions of people were out of work. After the fun of the Roaring Twenties, the country fell into a major **economic** slump and people struggled throughout the 1930s to make a living. Alfred was one of the many people trying to find a way to make money.

One of his ideas was a board game. He designed an **anagram** game with letters on wooden chips. As he was testing it, he hit a snag. Often, he'd get a random assortment of letters that wouldn't make a word. Inspired by Edgar Allen Poe's story "The Gold Bug," Alfred decided to balance the number of tiles for each letter based on how often each letter appeared in everyday English. To do this, he counted letters in *The New York Times* and other newspapers. He called his game *Lexico*.

No publishers were interested in *Lexico*, so he published it himself. By 1934, he'd only sold 84 sets. The game wasn't good enough, Alfred decided, and he set about improving it. Inspired by crossword puzzles, he divided his game board into squares, devised a point system, and added special squares to double or triple points. He finished his new game in 1938 and tried to sell it. He still had no takers! Alfred almost gave up.

There are many styles of *Scrabble* boards.
credit: thebarrowboy (CC BY 2.0)

sanction: to approve.

staple: something that is used often.

posh: expensive, upper class.

deduction: using logic or reason to figure out or form an opinion about something.

Then, in 1947, another man, James Brunot (1902–1984), bought the rights to the game. He spruced it up and changed the name to *Scrabble*. The game still floundered, and Brunot almost gave up, too. But, in 1951, Brunot got a rush of orders from a department store called Macy's—and soon had too many orders to handle. Brunot sold the manufacturing rights to a Long Island, New York, company that had previously rejected the game. By 1953, this company had sold 4 million copies of *Scrabble*! Eventually, the game was sold to Hasbro, the current maker of *Scrabble*.

Today, *Scrabble* is still extremely popular. One out of every three homes in America has a *Scrabble* set. And every year, tens of thousands of people compete in tournaments worldwide. The National Scrabble Association **sanctions** more than 175 tournaments a year, including the National Scrabble Championship.

CLUE / CLUEDO

In 1943, a British factory worker named Anthony Pratt (1903–1994) was bored. He was doing his part for the war effort by working at a factory. Evenings, though, were long and dull during World War II. Germany was bombing London, England. All houses and businesses had to be blacked out at night. Plus, gas and food were in short supply.

Mahjong

Mahjong is a tile game from China. A typical set includes 144 tiles in different suits, such bamboo, wind, and dragon. Many theories exist about the game's origin. Archaeologists have found tile games of some form that date back to at least 1120 CE in China. Mahjong didn't spread throughout China, though, until after 1905.

The Western world discovered the game after 1920. The game became popular in Asia, Britain, and the United States. Each developed its own variation of the game.

 You can learn how to play mahjong at this website.

⌕ learn mahjong 2.5 minutes

Poker

Poker is a family of card games that involves bluffing and betting. Historians are not quite sure of poker's roots. Some historians think the game goes back a thousand years. It may come from a domino-like game played in tenth-century China. Or poker may have evolved from a sixteenth-century Persian game called *As Nas*.

The word *poker*, though, probably comes from *Pogue*, a seventeenth-century French card game. The French brought the game to North America—New Orleans, Louisiana, in particular. English-speaking settlers turned *Pogue* into poker. By 1834, poker had evolved into the game we know today, in which players are dealt five-card hands from a 52-card deck and bet on the value of their cards. The game spread up the Mississippi River on riverboats and became a **staple** of saloons in the West. During World War I, American soldiers spread the game to Europe. As the decades passed, different variations of poker, including Texas hold'em and seven-card stud, evolved.

Anthony loved reading mystery novels, but they weren't enough to keep him busy. So, he decided to design a game—inspired by mysteries. Anthony and his wife studied the works of great British mystery writers, such as Agatha Christie (1890–1976) and the creator of Sherlock Holmes, Arthur Conan Doyle (1859–1930). They took the best ideas from the authors.

Anthony set the game in a **posh** country mansion and stocked it with a cast of characters and weapons. The players would be detectives trying to solve a murder. They would rely on logic and **deduction** to figure out the who, what, and where of the murder mystery. At first, Anthony called the game *Murder*.

By 1944, he had a game. It impressed a game publisher, but he didn't like the name. The publisher made a few other changes and agreed to publish the game as *Cluedo*. It's a blend of the words *clue* and *ludo*, which is Latin for "I play." *Cluedo* went on sale in Britain in 1949.

WORDS TO KNOW

promote: to make people aware of something, such as a new product, through advertising, or to make something more popular or well known.

mass market: products that are sold on a large scale.

American game maker Parker Brothers published the game as *Clue*. The game didn't sell well at first, but sales gradually gathered steam. By the 1970s, *Clue* was one of the most popular board games, alongside classics such as *Monopoly*, *Life*, and *Scrabble*. And it still is today!

DID YOU KNOW?

In 1985, *Clue* was made into a comedy movie with three different endings!

MODERN GAMES

In the mid-twentieth century, game companies such as Milton Bradley and Parker Brothers made hundreds of board games, mostly for families and kids. Adults tended to play classic games such as chess, bridge, and poker. But that started to change in the 1970s.

In 1979, Chris Haney (1950–2010) and Scott Abbott sat down to play *Scrabble*. But a few of the pieces were missing. What do you do when presented with this kind of roadblock? In their case, the two friends decided to invent their own game!

Chris and Scott created *Trivial Pursuit* that afternoon. In this game, players answer trivia questions to earn game pieces. For a couple of years, they raised money and worked on the game. In 1981, they printed about 1,100 *Trivial Pursuit* sets and sold them to stores.

Chris and Scott lost money because the games cost more to make than what they were sold for. They tried to sell the game to publishers, but were rejected. They almost gave up (does that sound familiar?), until they hit upon a novel way to **promote** the game. They asked celebrities mentioned in the game to help promote it. It worked! By 1984, Chris and Scott had sold 20 million copies of *Trivial Pursuit*, making it the fastest-selling board game in history. And a publisher eventually bought the game.

Trivial Pursuit paved the way for games such as *Pictionary* and other **mass market** party games in the 1980s and 1990s.

DUNGEONS & DRAGONS

In 1974, Gary Gygax (1938–2008) and Dave Arneson (1947–2009) invented a real game changer—and a whole new category of games. Both men loved war gaming. Gary had even designed a medieval war game called *Chain Mail*. But they were bored with the way war games were played, with players usually controlling whole armies.

War Gaming

People have been playing strategy and war games for thousands of years. Chess started as a war game. In the early twentieth century, war gaming emerged as a distinct type of hobby game. In it, players moved miniature soldiers on tabletop battlefields. They might reenact historical battles or fight fantasy wars. Today, games such as *Warhammer Fantasy Battle* remain popular.

WORDS TO KNOW

theme: a central, recurring idea or concept.

Eurogame: the term for board games designed in Europe, primarily in Germany.

Gary and Dave worked together to design a new type of game that combined war gaming and fantasy battles—*Dungeons & Dragons*! They tried to sell it a publisher, but no one was interested. So the two men formed their own game company, TSR.

In *Dungeons & Dragons*, players get to design and play their own heroes involved in ongoing fantasy adventures. Each player becomes one of characters—perhaps an elf taking part in a hunt for treasure. A leader, or dungeon master, guides players through the story.

With *Dungeons & Dragons*, role-playing games were born. In the following decades, *Dungeons & Dragons* spawned many competitors—but it remains the bestselling role-playing system.

Dungeons & Dragons tools of the game

What's in a Name?

Dungeons & Dragons could've been called *Swords & Spells* or *Magic & Monsters*. Originally, Gary Gygax and Dave Arneson just called it the *Fantasy Game*. But they knew they needed something better. They drew up a chart of fantasy elements and then picked a few that sounded good together. Gary's five-year-old daughter was the one who picked *Dungeons & Dragons*.

EUROGAMES

In the 1960s, the U.S. company 3M started making strategy games—and marketing them to Europe. 3M enlisted game designers Alex Randolph (1922–2004) and Sid Sackson (1920–2002) to design them. Their game, called *Acquire*, planted the seed that grew into a whole new kind of board game that's been dubbed European-style, or German-style. In *Acquire*, players invest in and take over companies, racing to acquire the most wealth.

These games sometimes have a **theme**, such as building railroads or settling new land. **Eurogames** also have short and clear rules, can be played in a reasonable amount of time, and do not eliminate players. Plus, you can't rely on luck!

TableTop with Wil Wheaton

From 2012 to 2017, *TableTop* was an influential web series on the Geek & Sundry YouTube channel. Created by Wil Wheaton (1972–) and Felicia Day (1979–), the show helped popularize modern board and card games. In every episode, Wil—who also starred in *Star Trek: NG* and *Big Bang Theory*—and his friends play a board, card, or role-playing game, such as *Settlers of Catan Star Trek* edition, *Munchkin*, or *Dread*. Why do you think people enjoyed watching other people play games?

PS You can watch *TableTop* here.

🔍 TableTop

WORDS TO KNOW

Vikings: a group of seafaring pirates and traders from Scandinavia who migrated throughout Europe between the eighth and eleventh centuries.

debut: to introduce.

SETTLERS OF CATAN

Game designer Klaus Teuber (1952–) was obsessed with **Vikings**—real Vikings. While they did do plenty of invading, they were also seafarers, craftsmen, traders, and even settlers. Teuber wondered what the Vikings needed to do to settle Iceland—and he turned it into a game.

Settlers of Catan

In the game, players trade and buy resources to build towns and roads on the fictional island of Catan. *Settlers of Catan* **debuted** in Germany in 1995. It quickly became the first German game to become a hit outside Europe. *Settlers of Catan* won the Spiel des Jahres that year. Since then, the game (and all of its expansions) have sold more than 20 million copies worldwide. Although the game industry had been thriving in Germany, *Settlers of Catan* helped breathe new life into the industry in other parts of the world.

TICKET TO RIDE

By the early 2000s, European-style games began influencing North American game designers. Alan Moon (1951–) was one of them. He'd won a Spiel des Jahres in 1998 for a game called *Elfenland*. He got the idea for his breakthrough game, *Ticket to Ride*, one day when he was walking along a beach in Massachusetts. He had an "aha" moment where the pieces of the game idea fell into place.

In *Ticket to Ride*, players compete to build and control railways across America. The prototype played well, and Moon sold the game to a game company called Days of Wonder. Moon won his second Spiel de Jahres for *Ticket to Ride* in 2004. The game has spawned numerous spinoffs and expansions, including settings in Europe, Germany, and Nordic countries, as well as in different time periods.

DID YOU KNOW? Alan Moon is one of only three non-German designers to have won a Spiel de Jahres since 1986.

The original version has sold more than 3 million copies so far.

WORDS TO KNOW

collectible card game (CCG): a type of strategy card game with specially designed cards that the player can collect to customize their deck; also called a trading card game.

deck building: a game mechanic where the player selects cards to build a custom set of cards.

rampage: uncontrolled and usually violent behavior.

COLLECTIBLE CARD GAMES

Magic: The Gathering, a **collectible card game (CCG)**, was another modern game changer. In 1993, Richard Garfield (1963–) designed this game for Wizards of the Coast. Wizards of the Coast was a small game company that specialized in role-playing games. Its founder wanted a portable game to sell. Garfield adapted an old idea he had for a card game—and the result was *Magic: The Gathering*. In the game, two wizards duel each other by casting spells and summoning creatures. *Magic: The Gathering* was first released at Milwaukee Game Con in 1993. It was a runaway success, selling out for two years!

DID YOU KNOW?

You can play *Magic: The Gathering* professionally. Imagine having that as your job!

Magic also created a new category of games—collectible card games.

Each card is a specific spell, creature, or land. Some cards are more powerful and rarer than others. And Wizards of the Coast also changes the cards through time. Every player starts off with a base deck of *Magic* cards. Then, they buy new cards or trade their cards for new cards to customize their deck. This created a new aspect to card games called **deck building**. Players can build their decks, stacking them with certain cards. Deck building even created styles of play. For instance, some players stack their decks with **rampaging** creatures, while others prefer powerful spells.

The enormous success of *Magic: The Gathering* spawned many other CCGs, including ones in the *Star Trek*, *Star Wars*, and *Pokémon* universes.

More than 150 years ago, a young Milton Bradley saved his printing business with a board game. It was a game changer that kicked off an industry. Since then, game designers and players in the United States, Europe, and all around the world have made tabletop games big business. And every once in a while, another game changer comes along and gives us whole new ways to play.

Why are games so popular? What keeps us going back for more? We'll explore the science behind gaming in the next chapter!

ESSENTIAL QUESTION

Why do people invent new games?

Pokémon Cards

Pokémon emerged as a gaming cultural phenomenon. Short for "pocket monsters," *Pokémon* started as a game for handheld consoles in 1996. In the same year, the *Pokémon* CCG debuted. Game play was based on the mechanics of *Magic: The Gathering*. Players can collect, trade, and battle different *Pokémon* cards. Some of the rarest cards can be worth tens of thousands of dollars! Two years later, *Pokémon* the television series hit Japan. Since then, *Pokémon* have starred in movies and a groundbreaking mobile game.

Activity

WHAT'S THE STORY?

You've probably played many more classic board games than we could cover in this book. Many probably have fascinating stories behind them. For instance, as you learned, the creator of *Clue* was inspired by British murder mysteries.

❯ **Research a classic board game not discussed in this chapter.**

❯ **Who invented it?** Why? What were his or her inspirations? Jot these answers down in your design notebook.

❯ **Has the game changed through the years?** What did the game look like originally? Sketch it in your design notebook.

❯ **Write a paragraph about the history of the game.**

❯ **If you have a copy of the game, play it!** How is the game played? Write out the goal of the game and its rules.

DID YOU KNOW?

In the newest version of *Clue* (2016), Mrs. White was killed off and replaced with Dr. Orchid. She's an expert in poisonous plants!

Try This!

Research the origins of a classic card game. What's the history of *Uno* or *Rook*, for instance? Do some games have similar stories of creation?

PIZZA BOX BATTLESHIP

What you need: two pizza boxes, 4 pieces of graph or plain paper, push pins

Battleship is a classic board game that's been around since 1967. People have been playing the pencil-and-paper version for much longer. The game is thought to be based on a French game from World War I. A player secretly positions ships on their side of the board and then takes turns guessing where their opponent's ships are.

❯ **Divide each piece of paper into an 11-by-11-inch grid.** You can also design the grid on a computer and print it out! Label the cells going down 1 through 10 and the cells going across A through J. Glue or tape a grid inside the top and bottom of each pizza box.

❯ **Open the pizza boxes and set the top lids back to back.** You may want to use a binder clip (or two) to keep the lids from falling.

❯ **Make two sets of different-sized ships out of construction or other paper.** Typical ships include the following.

* Carrier, covers 5 squares
* Battleship, covers 4 squares
* Cruiser, covers 3 squares
* Submarine, covers 3 squares
* Destroyer, covers 2 squares

❯ **To play, each player places their fleet of ships on the bottom grid.** Players take turns "firing" by guessing a square where they think one of the other player's ships is. For instance, one player calls out B7, and places a pin in B7 on his top grid. If the other player has a ship covering B7, they call out "hit" and place a push pin in that square. If not, they say "miss." The first player to sink all the opposing player's ships wins!

Try This!

Change the theme of the game. Instead of naval vessels, for instance, try making it a space battle game.

ROLE-PLAYING GAMES (RPGS)

Many local libraries offer RPG nights or clubs. The American Library Association even put together a list of free downloadable RPGs! Check them out at this website.

🔍 ALA
free RPG

❯ **Gather two or three friends.** You'll also need paper, pencils, and dice.

❯ **Research and pick one of the RPGs from the ALA's list.** *StickGuy*, for instance, is very simple and a great introduction to role playing.

❯ **Pick one person to be the game or dungeon master (GM).**

❯ **Follow the directions on how to create characters and a story.** Jot down your character's powers and other features in your design notebook. If you're the GM, write down the story.

❯ **Play the game!**

❯ **Does playing the game give you some ideas for a game you'd like to invent?** Jot those down in your design notebook.

Try This!

See if your local library has a role-playing club—and join in on the fun.

PLAY MOBILE (BOARD) GAMES!

Thousands of new games are released every year. And the rise in board and card games might be partly because of the internet. Many game companies have released online or mobile versions of their games, often for free or for a minimal cost. People often try out the app before buying the board game itself.

❯ **With an adult's permission, try out the mobile version of a modern board game.** You might try *Pandemic* or *Settlers of Catan*.

❯ **What does the game look like?** Sketch it in your design notebook.

❯ **How is it played?** Write out the game's goals and its rules.

❯ **Play the game with a friend or against the computer.** Was it fun? Why or why not?

❯ **Does it give you some ideas for a game you'd like to invent?** Jot those down in your design notebook.

DID YOU KNOW?
Some of the early *Monopoly* tokens doubled as prizes in Cracker Jack boxes.

Try This!

If you have a copy of a modern board game, compare it to the mobile app version. Which is more fun? Would you have adapted the game differently?

Chapter 3

YOUR BRAIN ON
GAMES

Humans have played games for thousands of years. Why do we like them? Psychologists have been interested in this question for decades. And game designers study why we play games—and what makes them fun—in order to build better games.

Some experts say games help us escape everyday life. Others say they help us learn. Most experts recognize these are not the only reasons we play games, though. It boils down to this: Games are fun. We play games not because we're trying to learn or escape. We play simply because we enjoy the experience.

We do get other things out of playing, such as learning, social skills, and more. But that's not why we play in the first place.

ESSENTIAL QUESTION

What are some reasons humans play games?

IN THE ZONE

WORDS TO KNOW

psychologist: a person who studies the mind and behavior.

flow: to move in a steady, smooth way; a state of mind where we feel and perform our best.

The idea of doing something just for the experience isn't new. In the 1970s, psychologist Mihaly Csikszentmihalyi (1934–) came up with the idea of **flow**. Flow is a state of mind where you become completely absorbed by what you're doing. Nothing else seems to matter. You're so focused that you forget about problems and everything else. You can even lose track of time. You lose yourself in the game. It's an amazing feeling. Today, we might call flow being "in the zone."

Flow doesn't just happen when we're playing games. Writers, musicians, and artists often experience flow when they're creating. Runners may feel in the zone as they move along a trail. Chefs decorating a cake might lose track of time as they focus on making tiny frosted swirls. And video gamers often lose themselves in an adventure.

Types of Fun

We all know when something is fun. But did you know that there are many different kinds of fun? Hard fun is that joy we get in doing something challenging. Simple fun is the opposite. During simple fun, we relax and do something mindless. Creative fun comes when we build or make something. Destructive fun happens when we destroy something. Exploratory fun is the joy of exploring the unknown. Designers think about all of these different kinds of fun when creating games!

WORDS TO KNOW

neuroscientist: someone who studies the development and function of the nervous system, which includes the brain, spinal cord, and nerve cells throughout the body.

electrode: a conductor through which electricity enters or leaves an object, substance, or region.

ventral tegmental area (VTA): a group of nerve cells in the midbrain responsible for releasing dopamine.

nucleus accumbens (NAc): a region of the brain relating to addiction.

neurotransmitter: a brain chemical that carries information throughout the brain and body.

dopamine: a neurotransmitter that produces feelings of pleasure.

serotonin: a neurotransmitter with a wide variety of functions in the body. It contributes to feelings of well-being and happiness.

BIOLOGY OF FUN

Doing something you like triggers what's called the reward center in your brain. This was discovered in 1954 by American psychologist James Olds (1922–1976) and Canadian **neuroscientist** Peter Milner (1919–2018) at McGill University. They implanted **electrodes** in an area of a rat's brain called the **ventral tegmental area (VTA)**. The rats then learned to push a lever to reward themselves with electric stimulation. The rats liked the feeling, and soon became addicted!

This reward center in our brains is really several circuits or pathways that connect a handful of structures deep in the brain. One pathway includes the VTA and the **nucleus accumbens (NAc)**. As the rats discovered, this pathway plays a role in reinforcing our behavior.

Whenever we do something rewarding, such as eat food or have fun, the VTA releases a **neurotransmitter** called **dopamine**. This is a chemical that helps control our brain's reward and pleasure centers. The chemical travels to the NAc, and results in a feeling of happiness. It basically tells your body the experience was good and to do it again!

The brain also releases dopamine along other pathways. These pathways go to areas of the brain that control emotions, attention and planning, movement, and even memory. Dopamine plays a role in helping us move our body and control emotions, as well as recognize and act on rewards.

The reward centers in the human brain

credit: Oscar Arias-Carrión1, Maria Stamelou, Eric Murillo-Rodríguez, Manuel Menéndez González and Ernst Pöppel. Substantially modified by Seppi333 (CC BY 2.0)

DID YOU KNOW?

The human brain has roughly 100 billion neurons, or nerve cells, in it. That's about the same as the number of stars in our galaxy!

Dopamine isn't triggered only when we play games. Lots of things make us happy, right? You experience a rush of dopamine when you are with people you love, when you are successful at something, when you watch a show or listen to a piece of music that you like, and many other things. What makes you happy?

Dopamine isn't the only chemical in our brain making us feel good. Another neurotransmitter called **serotonin** plays a major role in regulating our mood, as well as our sleep and learning.

WORDS TO KNOW

oxytocin: a chemical released by your body that makes you happy when you interact with people you like.

endorphins: a group of hormones released in the brain that reduce feelings of pain and improve mood.

pyramid of needs: a way to organize human needs into most-important and less-important categories.

Serotonin is responsible for that feeling of being full or satisfied. Studies have shown that low serotonin levels can lead to depression. Another chemical, **oxytocin**, helps us feel close to other people. And our bodies release **endorphins** when feeling stress, fear, or pain.

What does all of this have to do with playing games? At a basic level, playing a good game triggers the brain chemicals that make us happy, which means we want to play more of it.

There's also a deeper psychology of games. We might start playing because it's fun, but we keep playing games, at least certain ones, because we get something out of them. They appeal to our basic human needs.

DID YOU KNOW?

Tabletop games can help you relax and de-stress! A survey found that 64 percent of the people who responded bought board, card, or other non-violent, casual games to unwind. And 53 percent bought them for stress relief.

PSYCHOLOGY OF GAMES

Psychologist Abraham Maslow (1908–1970) described humans as having a **pyramid of needs**. At the bottom are basic needs such as food and shelter. Above that, we need to feel safe and secure. Then, we need to be loved and to belong. Next, we need to value ourselves, and, finally, we need to grow and be creative. Each level builds on the one below. For example, it's hard to be creative if you don't have enough to eat or a place to live.

Games appeal to those higher needs. To grow, we need to understand, explore, seek adventures, experience new things, feel excited, and so forth.

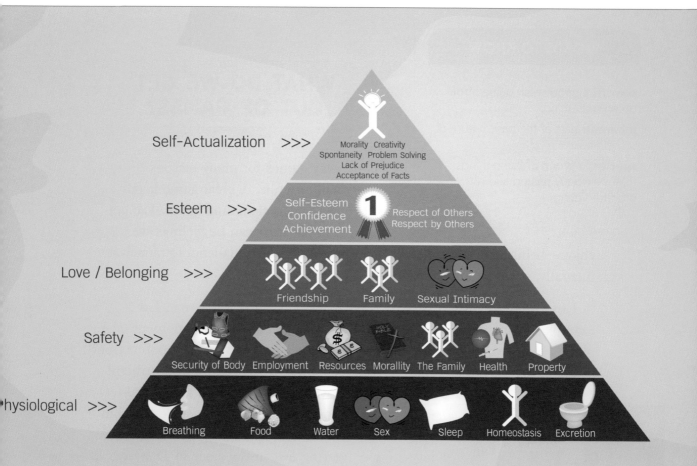

Abraham Maslow's pyramid of needs.

Games help us do many of these things right in our living rooms. Games offer competition, excitement, new experiences, and opportunities for make-believe. Players learn and use skills to beat opponents. They might even get to explore an alternate reality, such as a mythical world or a battlefield. And games are safe, despite what the *Jumanji* movies show! Players can feel like soldiers without being in danger of getting hurt.

Abraham Maslow came up with his pyramid in the 1940s. More recent psychologists have identified our needs as just three. We need to feel we are independent and have the power to make choices. We need to care about others and be cared for by them. And we need to feel good at what we do. These are all important needs to keep in mind when designing games, too!

WHAT DO WE GET OUT OF GAMES?

People play games for many reasons—other than just fun. A great game keeps you coming back again and again. We get something out it. It can be feelings we enjoy—being with other people, creating something, challenging ourselves mentally, or all of the above.

Emotional Payoff: A **payoff** is what you get out of the game. For example, the designers of *Cranium* built the game around the moment when players high-five each other. All the players get to feel funny or cool in front of their friends. Other games let you feel clever when you make a brilliant

College students playing charades in the 1950s

move or get a question right. You feel good when you make people laugh in charades or *Pictionary*. You might enjoy getting lost in the story in *Dungeons & Dragons*. Or you might like the thrill of victory when you conquer a continent in *Risk*. These are all emotional payoffs from games.

Socializing: We also play games to socialize. Does your family ever have a game night? Part of the fun of a good game is hanging out with friends and family. We feel as though we matter to these friends. Whether people are playing games around a kitchen table or online, the socialization aspect is an incredibly important part of playing games. It's also a chance to practice good sportsmanship. Have you ever seen someone get angry when they lose? What's a better reaction to disappointment? Why is losing well an important skill to have?

Gaming Addiction

Can you become addicted to games? The World Health Organization recognizes gaming disorder as an illness that involves abusing video and online games. Like most addictions, the symptoms include loss of control over gaming, making it more important that anything in your life, and continuing to do it despite any negative consequences. Don't worry, though. The disorder affects only a small number of gamers.

Some gamers become addicted to gambling. They have the urge to bet money or other things of value on the outcome of dice and card games. Gamblers with a problem do this despite negative consequences, even when they want to stop. In the normal brain, the reward system releases dopamine, a chemical that makes us feel good. Research suggests that the brains of addicts need more and more thrills to get the dopamine flowing. So, they gamble or game more and more, chasing that good feeling despite negative consequences.

Creativity: Playing games can be a way to express yourself. You might spin a great adventure for *Dungeons & Dragons*, build an unusual deck in *Magic: The Gathering*, come up with imaginative clues in *Codenames*, or ingeniously act out information when playing charades. While not everyone identifies as a creative person, humans are **inherently** creative—that's one reason our **species** has survived as long as it has! Games offer the opportunity for creativity that some people are not able to find in other areas of their lives.

Strategic Thinking: Some games give players the chance to outthink each other. They enjoy thinking several moves ahead in chess or *Go*. They might like putting together a plan of attack in *Risk* or a war game. The payoff comes when the plan works just as they thought it would.

Players might also love solving a mystery, such as who killed Mr. Boddy in *Clue*.

WORDS TO KNOW

metagame: all the elements of a game the player can participate in.

intuitive: having the ability to know or understand things without proof.

caudate nucleus: a structure in the brain that plays roles in different types of learning.

dementia: a group of brain diseases that cause the gradual decline in a person's ability to think and remember.

Alzheimer's disease: a form of dementia that grows worse through time and affects memory, thinking, and behavior.

Collecting: Many hobby game players enjoy collecting things, such as *Pokémon* cards or *Magic: The Gathering* cards. They might also do so to be part of a community of other players.

Designer Richard Garfield coined the term **metagame** to describe all the elements of a game the player can participate in. Metagame includes collecting, trading, discussing strategy, making deals, and practicing the game. All of these things add to the joy players get out of moving those pieces or laying down those cards or rolling those dice.

GOOD FOR YOUR BRAIN

New research suggests that board games are good for your brain. They make people better logical thinkers—and learners.

For example, playing chess may help you get higher math scores. During the 2008–2009 school year, researchers studied a group of middle school math students. Half the group got the usual instruction. The other half got the usual class, plus a 30-week chess training program. At the end of the year, the chess students got higher test scores and grades.

Where in the Brain?

The Riken Brain Science Institute scanned the brains of professional and amateur *Shogi* players. *Shogi* is a Japanese game similar to chess. Pro players spend hours a day playing the game, and they can make quick, **intuitive** moves. They also, as it turns out, use a different part of their brain to make very quick decisions! When given two seconds to make a move, an area in their brains called the **caudate nucleus** lit up. However, this wasn't the case with amateur players. And pros didn't use this area if they were given longer to decide. The researchers were surprised that the caudate nucleus was involved. Scientists originally thought the caudate nucleus controlled voluntary body movements. Now, though, they think this part of the brain might be associated with memory and learning. The caudate nucleus may enable pros to quickly recognize patterns on the board and come up with their next moves.

Board games may also keep our brains healthier when we get older.

In 2003, a study published in *The New England Journal of Medicine* found that older people who played board games or similar activities were less likely to get **dementia** or **Alzheimer's** disease. These are diseases of the brain that affect memory and reasoning. The researchers studied what a group of elderly people did for fun. The ones who played board and card games, did crossword puzzles, read, or wrote for fun were less likely to get dementia.

A French study looked at board game-playing for a longer period of time. They found that board game players were 15 percent less likely to develop dementia than non-gamers.

Game designers and developers have all of these things in mind when they start to work on a new game. In the next chapter, we'll learn more about the game-making process.

ESSENTIAL QUESTION

What are some reasons humans play games?

BEAD YOUR OWN NEURON

What you need: colored beads (70 beads total: 42 beads for dendrites, 10 for cell body, 12 for axon, 6 for the terminals) and flexible wire or thread.

When we play, our brain releases chemicals such as dopamine through specialized cells called neurons. Our brains are made up of billions of neurons! They send and receive signals using electricity and chemicals.

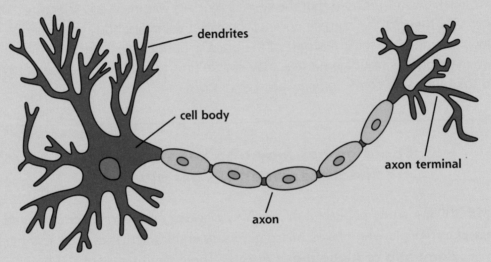

A neuron is made of a cell body, dendrites, axon, and the axon or synaptic terminal. The cell body is the core of the neuron. The dendrites and axon carry electrical signals. The synapses, which are the spaces between branches of the axon terminal, are where the axon terminal releases chemicals that travel to the next neuron.

In this activity, you're going to build your own neuron using beads!

❯ **Make the dendrites.** For this nerve cell, we'll make seven dendrites. For each, string six beads onto a short length of wire. Leave a little wire loose at the end of each so that you can attach the dendrites to the cell body.

❯ **Make the cell body.** String 10 beads of a different color than used for dendrites in a tight circle.

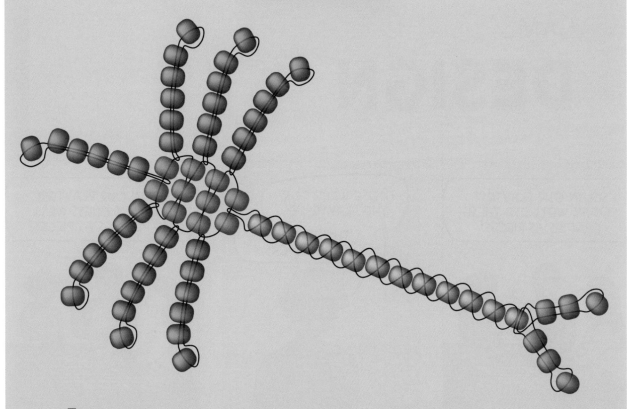

> **Attach the dendrites to the top and sides of the cell body.**

> **Make the axon.** String 12 beads together and then attach the axon to the bottom of the cell body.

> **Make the terminals.** For this nerve cell, we'll use two axon terminals. String three beads on each wire.

> **Attach the terminals to the end of the axon.** Now you have your own beaded neuron!

Try this!

Make another neuron, then do a little research. How would the two cells communicate? (Hint: The axon terminal contains the synapses where the chemicals are released.)

Chapter 4

GAME
DESIGN

Now that we've learned about the what and the why of games, let's take a look at the how. How do people come up with all these great games we love to play?

Professional game creators divide up the process of making a new game into design and development. The same person or team might do both. Often, though, different people design and develop the game. Designers come up with the game's **concept** and rules. Developers turn the concept into a publishable game.

Games all begin with an idea.

ESSENTIAL QUESTION

Where do ideas for games come from?

Designers can get ideas from anywhere. In 2003, a disease called **severe acute respiratory syndrome (SARS)** hit Hong Kong and then started to spread to Singapore, Beijing and Taipei in the Republic of China, and even Toronto, Canada. The World Health Organization dispatched a research team to deal with the outbreaks. The world watched the news, hoping that the outbreaks wouldn't turn into a pandemic. Luckily for everyone, they didn't. The research team found the source of the **virus** and halted the spread of the disease.

One of those people watching the news was game designer Matt Leacock. The potentially real pandemic gave him the idea for his game, *Pandemic*.

WORDS TO KNOW

concept: an idea.

virus: an extremely small particle that causes disease and is spread from person to person.

severe acute respiratory syndrome (SARS): a contagious and sometimes fatal respiratory illness that causes flu-like symptoms.

Playing *Pandemic*

WORDS TO KNOW

epidemic: a disease that hits large groups at the same time and spreads quickly.

iterative process: the process of arriving at a result through repeated rounds in which the product or idea is made a bit better in each round.

Not all game ideas have such a dramatic inspiration. Andrew Looney (1963–), the inventor of the Fluxx card games, says his game ideas usually just pop into his head. He likes to start with either a theme or a mechanic. For example, his idea for *Chrononauts* started with the thought, "I want to do a card game about time travel." On the other hand, for his game *Black Ice*, Looney wanted to make a game with a certain mechanic. He had a vision of a pyramid-shaped shell game. In *Black Ice*, players have to discover and unlock hidden codes under the pyramids to win.

Richard Garfield, the inventor of *Magic: The Gathering*, got the idea for one of his games while playing dice. He combined the mechanics of the classic game *Yahtzee* with the theme of Japanese monster movies to make *King of Tokyo*.

DID YOU KNOW?

Richard Garfield's advice to game designers: Play more games! They are great sources of inspiration and research.

Playing *Chrononauts*
credit: David Goehring (CC BY 2.0)

Cooperative Games

In most games, players compete against each other. In a cooperative game, though, players work together to achieve a goal. For instance, in *Pandemic*, players are part of a team of scientists battling **epidemics**. The team wins when all the diseases are cured. Everyone loses if a pandemic breaks out or the team runs out of time. Do you think cooperative games reflect real life, or are competitive games more realistic? Why?

THE DESIGN PROCESS

Most designers simply start off with an idea, try it out, and then keep tweaking the game until it works. The first part of this process involves coming up with and fleshing out the idea for the game. It usually includes not only the basic idea but also all the game's elements. Designers decide how you win the game, what pieces you use, what choices you must make, and what rules you need to follow!

Game design and development is an **iterative process**. Designers come up with an idea, build a prototype, test it, make changes—and then repeat the process again and again until the game is just right.

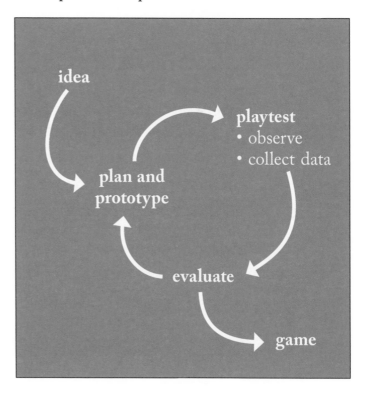

Game design begins with an idea—and those can come from anywhere. Matt Leacock got one from watching the news. Richard Garfield was inspired by playing other games. Game ideas can come from other fun activities, too, such as reading fantasy books, playing sports, traveling, watching movies, or telling stories.

Listen to this BBC interview with Matt Leacock.

(PS) What does he say about his game designing process?

🔎 BBC Matt Leacock

ELEMENTS OF A GAME

The basic elements of a card or board game include the space, components, mechanics, goals, and rules. Let's take a closer look at each of these.

Brainstorming Tips

Brainstorming is a terrific way to come up with game ideas. Often, this involves a small group of people quickly shouting out and writing down ideas. You can do this by yourself, too. Here are some tips.

> Don't stop with the first idea.

> Come up with many more ideas than you need.

> Treat every idea as a good one while brainstorming. In other words, no ideas are stupid! If you are in a group, that means ideas are not judged negatively.

> Don't get too attached to your ideas.

> Test out the ideas.

Space. All games happen somewhere. This includes both where the game is played and where it's set. For example, the traditional *Monopoly* game is played on a board. The game is set, though, in Atlantic City! All of the places in the game are named after streets in Atlantic City, New Jersey.

Clue is also a board game, but it's set in a mansion where a murder has taken place. *Magic: The Gathering* is a card game, but players imagine they're battling other sorcerers on the plains of the Multiverse. RPGs are played between players with no board or cards, but the settings are elaborate fantasy worlds.

DID YOU KNOW?

In *Monopoly,* one of the street names is misspelled! The most expensive of the yellow properties is called *Marvin* Gardens. The real place is *Marven* Gardens.

Monopoly components
credit: SarahDobbs (CC BY 2.0)

Some games don't necessarily have a setting. For instance, *Scrabble* or *Sorry* are simply games played on a board. Some games, though, may have lost their original setting through the years. For instance, we don't think of chess as being played anywhere other than a chessboard. Long ago, though, *Chaturanga*—the origin of chess—was set on a very different looking board.

DID YOU KNOW?

A meeple is a roughly person-shaped game token. Meeples are used in many European-style games, such as *Carcassonne*. The word is a combination of "my" and "people." Meeples can be made of wood or plastic.

Components. The pieces of a game are called components. They can include the board, cards, dice, counters, timers, tokens, money, puzzle pieces, tiles, maps, and even interactive elements such as apps. For example, the components of *Monopoly* include a folding game board, money, player tokens, houses, hotels, dice, and cards. *Settlers of Catan* includes cards, various tokens, and a game board made of individual hexagons. These let the players put the board together differently each time. A simpler game, such as *Uno*, includes just cards.

Mechanics. A game is really a series of interesting choices. Do you buy Park Place? Do you guess that Professor Plum murdered Mr. Boddy in the library with a pipe? Do you roll the dice to see if zombies attack? These choices are called mechanics. A game has a core mechanic as well as several smaller ones.

The online board game community, BoardGameGeek, keeps a list of game mechanics and explanations at this website. How many have you used while playing games? What might you use to build your own game?

🔍 PS

🔎 BoardGameGeek mechanics

Some common mechanics include acting, betting, rolling dice, bidding, attacking, eliminating players, building a pattern, placing tiles, trading, voting, and storytelling, to name just a few.

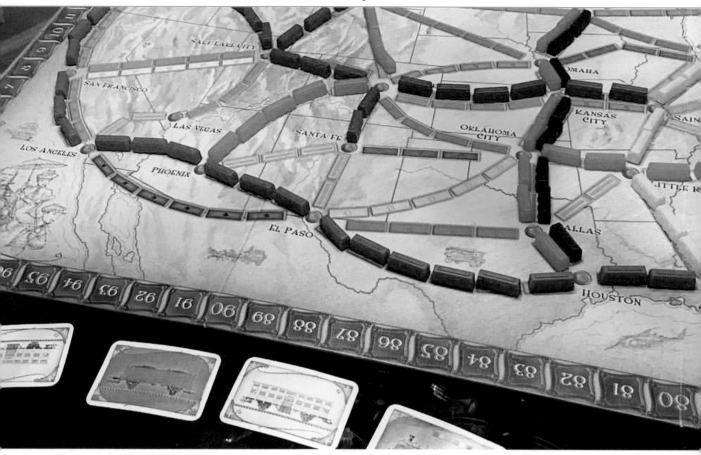

Ticket to Ride
credit: Greg Palmer (CC BY 2.0)

For instance, in *Ticket to Ride*, the mechanics include drawing and collecting a set of matching cards. In charades, the mechanic is acting out words and phrases. *Dixit* includes the mechanics of storytelling and voting.

The card game *Magic: The Gathering* introduced a new mechanic called tapping. Previously, designers hadn't thought about the idea of turning a card on or off! In the game, land cards must be tapped in order for the player to use their energy to cast spells. When a player taps a card, they turn it 90 degrees. Then, they can play a spell card or monster card. To use the tapped card again, the player has to first untap it and then tap it again in a later turn.

Many games use the mechanic of card drafting. With it, a player picks cards from a limited set in order to get an advantage over the other players.

resource: something that people can use.

settlement: a place where a group of people moves to start a new community.

DID YOU KNOW?

Some games use **resources** such as land, lumber, sheep, and even people. In *Settlers of Catan*, for instance, players collect cards with resources, such as wool, brick, lumber, and grain. They can turn in these resources to build roads, **settlements**, and cities.

For instance, in *Ticket to Ride*, the player can pick a card from a faceup set of cards. Selecting the right card can help the player build a railroad—and possibly prevent other players from building a railroad.

Goals. How do you win? Every game has a goal or victory condition. In *Clue*, the winner is the first player who figures out who the murderer is, what weapon was used, and the room where the murder took place. In *Uno*, you win if you're the first to play all your cards, provided you remember to say "Uno!" In *Pandemic*, though, everyone wins if they cure all the diseases. Remember, *Pandemic* is a cooperative game, where all players work together toward a goal.

Rules. How do you play? The rules pull the elements of the game together. The rules tell players how to play the game and what moves are allowed and what moves are not allowed.

Press Your Luck

This mechanic goes by several names. With it, players can repeat a risky action until they decide to stop—or suffer some consequence. The action should have the potential for a really big payoff, such as winning the game. But the action can also seriously backfire. For instance, the goal of blackjack is to have cards that add up to 21—or as close to it without going over 21. Players can press their luck by asking for more cards. They might hit 21—or they might go over, losing the game. Do you like to take such risks in games?

In most games on the market, the rules usually cover the contents of the box, an overview of the game, setup instructions, the goal of the game, and steps for playing and scoring. Clear rules are very important!

DESIGN PRINCIPLES

Game Design Tips

› Make the game shorter, if you can.

› Include some element of luck— but not too much!

› Balance luck and strategy.

› Include a catch-up feature.

› Have someone test your rules.

Think about what makes a game fun. A fun game isn't too long or too short. It doesn't rely solely on luck or skill. And it seems fair. Plus, it's balanced between challenging and not too hard. Those are just a few of the design principles that designers keep in mind. Let's take a closer look at these.

Play length. When designing a game, play length, or the time it takes to play the game, is an important consideration. If it's too short, the game might not be satisfying. If it's too long, the game might get boring or tiring. What is the right length for a game? That depends on the game and the players. A hand of *Uno* might take just 15 minutes. However, a more complicated game, such as *Monopoly* or *Dominion*, might take hours to play. And a *Dungeons & Dragons* campaign may take days. Those games need to take longer to be fully enjoyed.

However, most board designers like to err on the side of shorter games.

Luck vs. Strategy. Games of luck are based on chance. Strategy games let players outthink each other. Some games, such as chess and *Go*, rely nearly 100 percent on strategy. Other games, including *Bunco*, are 100-percent luck. Most players, though, like games that include both luck and strategy.

The hard part is finding the perfect balance. Having an element of luck—such as rolling dice or picking cards—in a board game makes players feel as though they don't have to agonize over every move or choice they make. Too much luck, though, makes players feel as though their thinking skills don't matter.

Fairness. Some games don't seem fair because a player might get eliminated early or one player can run away with the game. For example, in *Monopoly*, one lucky player might get so wealthy that it's impossible for the other players to catch up. And that's not fun, at least for the other players.

> Many European-style games keep all players in the game until the end. Also, many games now include a catch-up feature.

This makes it possible for anyone to win right up until the end of the game. For instance, *Scrabble* includes bonuses for using all of your tiles in one word. *Settlers of Catan* has the Robber. He can be played to stall whoever's in the lead, giving others a chance to catch up.

WRITE IT DOWN!

Game designer Andrew Looney jots down his ideas in a design notebook. When he gets a good idea, he writes a design memo. The act of writing down the idea helps him figure out if it's really as good as he thought it was. If it is a good idea, he keeps working on the concept.

Microgames

A microgame is a small board, war, or card game with few components. These games are designed to be played quickly. For instance, *Love Letter* has 16 cards and a few tokens. A round can be played in a few minutes. There isn't a standard definition of how small is small, though. *Coin Age*, for example, has just one card and a few coins. Don't be fooled by a microgame's size, though. Many—including *Love Letter*, *Coup*, and *Coin Age*—have won awards and can be played over and over again.

Game Designer Alan Moon

Best known for the game *Ticket to Ride*, Alan Moon is one of the few designers who's won the Spiel des Jahres twice. He won for *Elfenland* in 1998 and *Ticket to Ride* in 2004. Born in England, he and his family moved first to Canada and then New Jersey. When he was kid, Alan played many classic board games, his favorite being *Risk*. During college, he started a game club called the Jersey Wargamers. After college, he worked for several game companies, including Avalon Hill, Parker Brothers, and Ravensburger, a German game and toy company. Today, Alan is a **freelance** game designer who has designed more than a dozen games.

Once a designer works out the concept, they typically describe the game in a document. These documents vary from designer to designer and game company to game company. No matter what they look like, though, the documents help other people working on the game to understand its goal and rules. This is essential for the next phase of game creation: development. Can you think of other projects that work best when you document every step of the way?

ESSENTIAL QUESTION

Where do ideas for games come from?

Games start with an idea— and a design problem.

The problem might be how to make a card game about time travel or a cooperative board game about epidemics. The designer then brings together different game elements and design principles to solve that problem. The result is a game design.

At this point, the game might just be some notes in the designer's notebook. In the next part of the process—game development—the designer tests and changes the idea to make it work. We'll tackle this in the next chapter.

WHAT'S THE PAYOFF?

When we play games, we get something out them. Maybe you love the thrill of outthinking an opponent. Maybe you love working together in a group to solve a puzzle or you love making people laugh. In this activity, you'll explore more about the payoff from playing games.

❯ **Pick one of your favorite games.** Play it with friends. Which parts do you enjoy the most? Which did your friends enjoy?

❯ **What's the payoff of this game?** Write this in your design notebook.

❯ **Do a little research.** Which other games have this same payoff? Would you like to design a game with this payoff? Why or why not?

Game Designer Susan McKinley Ross

Susan Ross is a game and toy designer best known for the award-winning game, *Qwirkle*. She had the idea for the game in a dream! She'd been watching people play *Scrabble*. A couple mornings later, she woke up with the idea for *Qwirkle*. It's a tile game that uses colors and shapes instead of letters.

 You can listen to an interview with Susan about how she designed *Qwirkle*.

🔎 ideaduck Qwirkle

Try This!

Play another game you really like. Does it have the same payoff?

BOARD GAME MASHUP

One Hasbro designer said he often sees ideas as mashups. A game might get pitched as *Scrabble* meets *Connect 4*. What would that game look like? How does mashing up two games create something entirely new and fun? In this activity, you'll mash up two games to create a new one.

❯ **Pick out a couple of classic board or card games.** For example, you might pick *Yahtzee* and *Battleship*.

❯ **Take one or two elements from one game and add it to the other.** For instance, you could take the dice from *Yahtzee* and add it to *Battleship*. How might that change *Battleship*?

❯ **Write some new rules for the game that include the new element.** For instance, you could roll the dice in *Battleship* to select how many shots you get to fire or which row you pick.

❯ **Play the game with the new rules and elements.** How did that change the game? Did it give you any ideas for a new game? Write the ideas in your design notebook.

DID YOU KNOW?

Matt Leacock got his idea for *Pandemic* from an outbreak of disease. He donates 5 percent of the **royalties** from *Pandemic* games to Doctors Without Borders. This charity sends doctors to areas around the world that need medical assistance. In 2014, *Pandemic* players raised $50,000 for this charity to fight **Ebola** in western Africa.

Try This!

Mash up a few more elements! Or try the activity with two new games, such as *Uno* and *Monopoly*.

WORDS TO KNOW

royalty: money paid to the creator of something for every unit sold.

Ebola: a virus that causes a rare and deadly disease.

77

COMPARE TABLETOP GAMES

Board game shows abound on YouTube, and they are a great way to check out games you don't have and might like to buy. More than most, Wil Wheaton's *TableTop* on Geek & Sundry has helped popularize modern board and card games. In every episode, Wheaton and friends play a tabletop game, such as *Star Trek Catan*, *Munchkin*, or *Formula D*. Many other shows also demonstrate how to play specific games.

❯ **With permission from an adult, pick out a couple of episodes of *TableTop* that demo two games you'd like to try.** Think about the kinds of games you usually enjoy, as this will help you decide.

❯ **Watch the episodes, paying close attention to each game's space, goal, mechanics, components, and rules.** Write these in your design notebook for each game.

❯ **Which game elements did you really enjoy?** Did they give you any ideas for your own game? Jot those down in your design notebook!

❯ **Write a brief paragraph comparing the two games.** How are they similar? How do the different elements make for different experiences?

Try This!

Watch a few more episodes! This time look for cool and unusual themes for games. For instance, the theme of *Azul* is laying tiles in a Spanish court. *Codenames* is about spies. *Steam Park* is about amusement parks. Are there any themes you'd like to design a game around? Are there any that no one has done before? This is your chance to be really creative, to brainstorm, and to let your imagination carry you wherever it goes.

GAMIFY THE FUN

Some designers have based games on an experience they loved, such as going to an amusement park, telling stories, or watching a scary movie.

▶ **Think of a fun experience, such as something you really enjoyed doing in the past or something you still enjoy doing.** It can be anything: playing dodgeball, running a race, eating your favorite food, or watching a space adventure movie. This will be the theme and/or setting of your game!

▶ **Think about how you might make the game work.** Consider the following.

- How would you win?

- What mechanics would you use?

- What components does the game have? Is it a board or card game?

- What are the rules?

▶ **Now write a brief description of your game in your design notebook.**

Try This!

Think again, and pick some random components or mechanics for your game!

Massively Multiplayer Thumbwrestling!

Everyone knows how to thumbwrestle. But have you tried thumbwrestling an entire audience?

 Watch this fabulous TED talk and give it a try with your friends.

🔍 TED massive thumbwrestle

MAKE A GAME #1: RANDOM GAME GENERATOR

Now, it's time to work on creating your own game! The following activities build on each other to guide you through the process of making a game. Sometimes, writers turn to writing prompts and random story generators (found online) to help spark their creativity. Let's try it with board games! You're going to make a paper version of a random game generator. You'll just need some dice and paper. If you're using one d6 (a die with six sides), list six items in the first three steps. If you using two d6, list 12. If you're using a d20, list 20.

❯ **List and number the themes you'd like to explore.** For instance, vampires, castles, haunted houses, baseball, fairytales, sunflowers, or something completely different.

❯ **List and number the game mechanics you'd like to use.** For instance, storytelling, press your luck, deck building, or something else.

❯ **List and number your game components.** Ideas include board, cards, and dice.

❯ **Roll the die (or dice) separately to pick the theme, core mechanic, and one component of your game.** For instance, you might end up with a vampire-themed storytelling game that uses cards!

❯ **Design that game!** What's the victory condition? How do you play? What other components does it use? What are the rules?

Try This!

Repeat the randomizer, only this time design either a card game or an RPG.

MAKE A GAME #2: STATE THE PROBLEM!

Coming up with an idea is just the beginning of the design process. As in other types of design, the purpose of game design is to solve a problem. If you're designing a bridge, for instance, the problem is how to get cars, trucks, and buses across an obstacle, such as a river. In a game, your design problem is more fun. Give it a try!

▶ **Consider a few different design problems.** You can use the ideas you came up with in your random game generator or think of something completely different. The problem might be, "How do I make a card game about circus performers that teens will like?" Or, "How do I make a board game that teaches kids to code?"

▶ **After you come up with a great idea, write a very short problem statement in your design notebook.** What problem will your game design solve? Try to make your statement clear and to the point. You can embellish your problem statement later as you think more about the game.

▶ **After writing your problem statement, try it out on friends or family.** What do they think of your idea?

DID YOU KNOW?

In 1962, a University of Illinois student invented the game *Operation*. It was part of a class assignment to invent a game or toy.

Try This!

Pick another idea and write a problem statement. Do different problem statements lend themselves to different kinds of games? Can you start to imagine what the final game will look like and play like?

MAKE A GAME #3: WRITE THE RULES!

Rules are essential for playtesting a game. The testers need to be able to play the game without having you there to explain it to them. Most rules include what comes in the box, how to set up the board or deal the first hand, who goes first, what happens in each turn, how to win, and how to keep score.

❱ **Find an existing board or card game similar to the one you're designing.** This might take some thought and persistence. Sources beyond your own game collection might include the library, your school, the game collections of friends, or, with the permission of an adult, the internet.

❱ **Study its rules—and what it includes.** For instance, does it include a sample round of play? What's confusing? What might you do differently?

❱ **Write your rules.** Be sure to include instructions for setting up the game, playing the game, and winning the game.

❱ **Test your rules.** Can you follow the directions? Did you leave out a step? If so, revise them and retest. Remember, having too many instructions can be just as problematic as having too few.

DID YOU KNOW?

Game designers actually play their games during all stages of the design and development process.

Try This!

Have someone else read your rules and give you feedback! What did they notice that you missed the first time around?

WORDS TO KNOW

playtest: the process of testing a new game for bugs and design flaws before bringing it to market.

Chapter 5

GAME DEVELOPMENT AND
BEYOND

Now that you've learned what goes into thinking up new games, let's look at how these games go from ideas to actual games you can play. After all, there's no fun in a game that stays in someone's head or a designer's notebook!

ESSENTIAL QUESTION

Why are game design and game development considered different parts of the game-making process?

Dominion developer Dale Yu thinks of his job as being similar to that of a book editor. He takes what the designers submit and tries to make the best game possible, similar to the way editors take a manuscript from a writer and try to make it the best book possible.

marketing: communicating in different ways to make a business known.

product engineer: a person who designs and develops something that will be sold.

manufacturing: making large quantities of products in factories using machines.

distribution: the way a product is divided up or shipped out to stores.

Developers work out all of the kinks by playtesting and revising the game. One way developers do this is by trying to break the game. What?! Why would they want to break a game? Wouldn't they want to make it better?

Trying to break a game actually does make it better. Developers push the game mechanics and rules to the limit, playtesting them over and over to make sure the game works well.

Game design and development are part of a loop.

Design documents are crucial for the process.

Look back at the image on page 67 in Chapter 4. Designers come up with an idea, build a prototype, test it, make changes—and then repeat the process again and again until the game is just right.

Remember the design document started by the game designer? This document survives throughout the development process. It is a way for the development team to understand what the designer intended. The development team might include game developers, playtesters, writers, artists, managers, **marketing** people, and **product engineers**.

For managers and marketing people, the designer might simply write a short description of the game. For the rest of the team, though, the designer would describe the game mechanics, rules, components, and other aspects in great detail. This information will help the development team test, revise, and produce the game!

Let's look at the different parts of game development—prototyping, playtesting, publishing (which includes **manufacturing**, **distribution**, and retail) and marketing.

DID YOU KNOW?

Many developers use common *Magic: The Gathering* cards to prototype games that use cards. *Magic* players tend to discard cards that are less valuable.

PROTOTYPING

In the first step of the process, developers build a prototype of the game—maybe even several prototypes. A prototype is a simple version of the game that can be tested out. The prototype should include the game's rules and components. It can be made of paper, cardboard, or even pieces of other games. For instance, a card game developer might make a prototype using paper printouts or labels pasted onto old playing cards. Dale Yu, for example, used plastic card sleeves in his *Dominion* prototype.

A developer might build several different prototypes, adjusting them as they're tested.

Although game development shops sell components for prototyping, most developers collect their own supplies from other sources. You can make your own prototyping kit with some of these items:

A paper prototype of a game called *Diamond Trust of London*, designed by Jason Rohrer

- Old playing cards
- Card sleeves
- Labels (full page, name tag, and address)
- Paper of all colors and weights
- Dice
- Tokens and similar pieces from other games
- Plastics cubes and chips (from teacher supply stores)
- Bags and baggies (sandwich and snack size)
- Boxes

Tabletop Simulator

Developed by Berserk Games, *Tabletop Simulator* is a virtual game-testing program. Developers can use it to playtest tabletop games online by uploading their own artwork and then playtesting remotely.

 You can take a look at *Tabletop Simulator* at this website, though to play the games requires purchasing the service.

🔎 Berserk Tabletop Simulator

Playtesting a game
credit: Tikva Morowati (CC BY 2.0)

PLAYTESTING!

Playtesting is a crucial part of game development, one that new designers often skip. During this phase, people play the game over and over again using the prototype. Playtesting allows designers and developers to step back from their game and see its strengths and weaknesses through someone else's eyes—someone who has never played the game before. To designers and developers, the elements and rules of a game may seem obvious because they're so familiar with what they created. But to someone new to the game, those rules may not be at all obvious—and may even be confusing or not fun!

For example, the inventor of *Pirate's Cove*, Paul Randles (1965–2003), playtested his first game hundreds of times. This helped him perfect the game and really understand how people played it.

packaging: the wrapper and all the parts of a container that holds a product.

investor: a person who gives a company money in exchange for future profits.

crowdfunding: a way of raising money for a project that involves many people each contributing a small amount.

Often, designers and developers will playtest the game themselves first—and make changes. Then, they'll get players to test out the game. Sometimes, they even hire people to do this—does this sound like a dream job? Playtesters often get paid in game copies. Testing is usually done several times at different stages of game development. For example, developers might playtest before the rules are finalized just to see if the game mechanics are fun. Later playtests work out issues with game play and the rules. Some playtesting may even focus on how the **packaging** looks! Why do you think all these types of playtests are important?

What happens during a playtest? As a group plays the game, the development team watches them play and takes notes. Developers may also interview the players after each game. Based on what they learn, the designers will make changes to the game—and then playtest it again. Developers keep doing this until the game is fun and playable.

Self-publishing

Game developers can also produce a game by self-publishing—they publish the game themselves. This means they have to do all the work a game company might do! The designer needs to find funding, produce the artwork, get the game board and pieces manufactured, find distributors, and market the game. Self-publishing is basically like running your own business!

PUBLISHING

How does a game go from a prototype to a glossy box sitting on a store shelf? There are actually several routes. Some designers and developers may work for a game company, large or small. In that case, the company publishes and markets the game. A small company might need to raise money through **investors** to do this.

However, many designers work for themselves. They might design and develop a game and then pitch it to a game company. Remember Matt Leacock? He got his start licensing *Pandemic* to a game company. In either case, the game company takes care of manufacturing and distributing the game.

Manufacturing. After the developers have honed the game, the company sends it to its art department. There, graphic designers polish the artwork and writers edit the rules.

The art department also designs the packaging.

Once the graphic design is finished, the game goes to the production people. They select the materials for the game board, pieces, and packaging. Production takes the computer files generated by the art department and has them printed.

Board games on display at a café
credit: Gary Sproul (CC BY 2.0)

What happens once the game starts rolling off the production line?

Distribution. A game company doesn't usually sell directly to stores or **consumers**. Companies called **distributors** buy many copies of the game from the game company. Generally, these distributors pay **wholesale** prices or even below-wholesale prices. The distributor stocks the game in its warehouses, takes orders from stores, and then ships copies of the game to these stores.

Retail. Today, two kinds of **brick-and-mortar** stores generally sell tabletop games. Small hobby or game shops tend to stock hobby games, such as *Magic: The Gathering*, *Dungeons & Dragons*, and *Warhammer*. Big-box stores such as Walmart and Target tend to sell mass-market board games, such as *Monopoly* and *Scrabble*, as well as more popular hobby games, including *Settlers of Catan* and *Pandemic*. Online giants, such as Amazon and eBay, sell all kinds of board and card games.

Kickstarter

In the early 2000s, European-style games such as *Carcassonne* and *Settlers of Catan* created demand for more cool and interesting games. But developing them and getting them to market was hard—until Kickstarter came along. Founded in 2009, Kickstarter is a crowdfunding site for creative projects. It was originally developed to fund music and film projects, but game developers soon discovered it. They can post a polished game prototype and request interested gamers to fund the project. In 2017, the average successful tabletop game raised more than $65,000 on Kickstarter. This crowd-funding site has revolutionized tabletop games by making it possible for more game developers to create and publish their games.

MARKETING

In order to sell a game, designers and companies have to think about who is going to buy it. Former game designer Brian Tinsman divides the board game market into four categories: mass-market, hobby games, American specialty, and European.

Mass-market games are popular classic, family, and party games that are usually found on the shelves of big stores. These games include *Monopoly*, *Scrabble*, *Taboo*, *Boggle*, *Cranium*, and most kids' games. You probably have some of these games at home.

Hobby games are more complex. Fans may play these games often and regularly buy new cards, figurines, and expansions for the game. Roleplaying, war gaming, and collectible card games fall into this category.

American specialty games are American games that aren't mass-market or hobby games. These include strategy, sports, and mystery games. *Apples to Apples* is a popular example of an American specialty game. In this game, players take turns judging each other's choices for inclusion in certain categories.

European games, as we discussed earlier, originate mostly from Germany. These games tend to be more strategic and thoughtful than mass-market games. Today, many non-European game designers and companies produce European-style games. Some popular European or European-style games include *Settlers of Catan*, *Carcassonne*, *Ticket to Ride*, *Pandemic*, and *Puerto Rico*.

All of these different types of games are marketed to audiences through various types of media. These include television, magazine, newspaper, and online advertising.

Game companies spend quite a lot of money researching ways to get the word out about their games.

Can you think of any game advertisements you've seen lately? What were they like? Do you think they were convincing? Did you want to buy the game after watching?

One game designer compared developing a game to sculpting. When designing a game, he'd cram everything he could think of into that game. But, during development, particularly during playtesting, he trimmed away all the excess stuff to reveal a great game that works.

Codenames

One of the best new party games of recent years is Czech Game Edition's *Codenames*. Designer Vlaada Chvátil (1971–) came up with the idea at a gaming event and even playtested it that day.

Codenames is a deceptively simple word-association game. Two teams of players give their team members one-word clues to help them uncover the codenames of their own secret agents. Vlaada believes the player experience is more important than the game's theme or mechanics. *Codenames* forces players to use both their imagination to connect words together and their social skills to make sure their teammates can get the clue. *Codenames* won the Spiel des Jahres in 2016. Have you ever played it?

Gloomhaven

Gloomhaven is a success story no one could have predicted, least of all its designer, Isaac Childres. It's a massive, cooperative fantasy board game that got its start on Kickstarter. In September 2015, Isaac took to Kickstarter to raise money to develop the game. His goal was to raise $70,000. People could pledge $79 in exchange for getting the game once it was produced.

Twenty-eight days later, nearly 5,000 people had backed the game and Isaac had raised nearly $400,000! He used the money to develop and produce *Gloomhaven*. A year later, he, along with game company Cephalofair Games, delivered the huge game to backers—it weighed 20 pounds! The game company also produced 2,000 additional copies for retail stores. Only there was a problem. Customers had pre-ordered 25,000 copies from retailers. They'd heard how good the game was and wanted copies. The game was selling for up to $500 on eBay! Cephalofair had to reprint the game, and, as of 2018, *Gloomhaven* was in its fourth reprinting.

Prototyping and playtesting —repeatedly—is all about getting the game ready for people to buy it.

ESSENTIAL QUESTION

Why are game design and game development considered to be different parts of the game-making process?

We've looked at some pretty amazing games that are available to play right now. What about the future? What kinds of games are we going to be laying out on the kitchen table in the years to come? We'll look at some ideas in the next chapter!

MAKE A GAME #4: MAKE A PAPER PROTOTYPE

Before game developers build a board and all the other components of the game, they often test the idea out on paper first. The goal at this stage is just to find out if the concept is fun—and worth pursuing.

▶ **Draw the board for your game on paper.** You can also design it on a computer and print it out on plain paper.

▶ **Assemble the game pieces you need.** You can use items from around the house, such as coins or paperclips. Or you can borrow game pieces from games you own. (You'll make some pieces in later activities!)

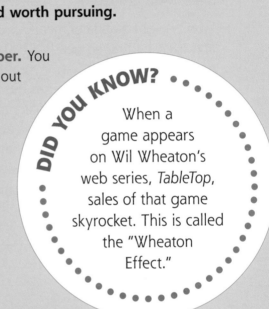

DID YOU KNOW?

When a game appears on Wil Wheaton's web series, *TableTop*, sales of that game skyrocket. This is called the "Wheaton Effect."

▶ **Write out the rules for your game.** Be very specific. At this point it's better to write too much than too little.

▶ **Recruit some friends to playtest your game.** Have them read the rules and then play your game!

▶ **Observe what works and what doesn't.** Write your observations in your design notebook.

▶ **Make changes to your game and the rules.** Repeat the playtest!

Try This!

Interview your friends to see what they liked and didn't like about the game. Write this in your design notebook.

MAKE A GAME #5: MAKE MEEPLES

Meeples are a type of game token used in many European-style games, such as *Carcassonne*. Meeples usually represent people in a game. They can be workers, armies, settlers, or something else. The word *meeple* is a combination of "my" and "people." Other game tokens can represent money earned, property bought, lands conquered, disease outbreaks, and more.

❯ **Design your meeple.** In most games, meeples look like miniature gingerbread men or women. Yours can look however you like! Typical meeples range from about ½-inch to 1½-inches tall. Yours can be any size of your choosing.

❯ **Draw the meeple shapes on stiff paper, such as card or chipboard.** You may also draw the meeples using a computer program and then print them out on cardstock. Many printers can handle thicker paper.

❯ **For each meeple, cut out several of the shapes.**

❯ **Glue the shapes together in layers until each meeple is thick enough to stand up.** Make as many meeples as you might need for your game.

❯ **If you used chipboard or cardstock that was one color, paint your meeples!** This allows you to add detail to your game tokens.

Try This!

Make many more types of tokens in this way, such as a coin or a hexagon or anything else you need for your game.

MAKE A GAME #6:
MAKE A GAME BOARD

Most tabletop games have a game board. When designers make a prototype, they sometimes draw the game board on paper for initial playtests. For later ones, though, designers might make a board out of chipboard.

> **Design your game board.** For this activity, the board should fit on one 8½-by-11-inch piece of paper. You can draw it on the paper or print it out from a computer.

> **Cut some poster board or chipboard to the same size as the paper board, plus an extra quarter-inch all around.**

> **Glue the back of the paper game board to the chipboard.** Carefully smooth out the glue so there are no wrinkles in your game board.

> **Carefully stick some contact paper to the back of the game board.** Smooth out any air bubbles and trim the edges.

> **Put binding or duct tape along the edges of the board.** This will make a nice edge all the way around your board.

> **Now you have a sturdy game board!**

Try This!

Design a *folding* game board that fits on two sheets of 8½-by-11-inch paper. Follow the above directions—except before you put the binding tape on the edges, use the binding tape (on the underside) to join the two sides together. Leave a small gap so the board will fold in half. Why is a portable game convenient?

MAKE A GAME #7: MAKE CARDS

In Chapter 1, you learned how to make playing cards with block-printed backs. This time, you're going to make cards for your board game. You'll prototype like the pros!

❯ **Design the faces of the cards you need for your game.** You can do this using a computer and then printing them out or you can draw each by hand.

❯ **Cut out each card face.** They should be the same size or smaller than a standard playing card.

❯ **Insert your cards into card sleeves so that the face is visible.** Then place a playing card behind the card within the sleeve. Adding the playing card makes your card stiff enough to shuffle and deal.

DID YOU KNOW?

In 2013, Wil Wheaton and Felicia Day held the first International Tabletop day. During it, they played numerous board games online. By the next year, the event spread worldwide with participants in 80 countries.

❯ **If you don't have card sleeves, glue a discarded playing card to the back of each of your cards.** Low-value *Magic* cards or cards from a deck of regular playing cards are options.

❯ **Shuffle and deal your cards!** You're ready to playtest.

Try This!

If you'd like to use smaller cards for your board game, try using business cards!

MAKE A GAME #8: PLAYTEST, PLAYTEST, PLAYTEST!

After you construct the game board, cards, meeples, and other tokens you might need, you're ready to playtest! If you need other components, such as dice or spinners, scavenge them from other games you own.

❯ **If you haven't done so already, make sure that the rules of the game are clear.** Set up the game components.

❯ **Invite some friends or family members to play.** Have your testers read the rules and then play the game.

❯ **As they play, note anything that isn't clear or doesn't seem to work.** Jot that in your design notebook.

❯ **Interview the players after a round.** How did they like the game? What didn't they like? Did they understand the rules? What worked well? What didn't work for them?

❯ **Make changes to your game.** Playtest again!

Try This!

Once you've playtested the game a few times and made adjustments, invite some new people to playtest it. Again, see if they can follow your written rules without you explaining anything!

MAKE A GAME #9:
MAKE A GAME BOX

First impressions often make a big difference in how a game is received. In later stages of playtesting, game developers often craft the packaging for the game. Not only does this keep the pieces together, but developers can also test out whether players like the way the game looks.

❯ **Pick out a gift box that's big enough to fit your game board and pieces.** You can find inexpensive gift boxes at a dollar store if you don't have any around the house.

❯ **Design the cover for your box.** You can draw and letter it by hand or design it on a computer and print it out. Depending on the size of the box, you might have to create and assemble it in sections.

❯ **Cut out chipboard to fit inside the lid and bottom of the gift box.** You can also cut out rectangular strips for the inner sides of the box.

❯ **Glue the chipboard to the inside of the gift box to make the box sturdy.**

❯ **Glue your artwork to the outside of the box.**

❯ **Put your game pieces in the box.**

DID YOU KNOW?

Scrabble is an official sport of several African countries, including Senegal and Mali.

Try This!

Using leftover chipboard, make dividers for the interior of the box. You can use the sections to store game pieces. Can you find existing games that do this well?

Chapter 6

THE FUTURE OF
GAMES

Humans have been playing cards, dice, and board games for thousands of years. Tabletop games are more popular than ever—despite digital alternatives, such as video games. Every once in a while, a game changer comes along and creates a whole new type of tabletop game, such as CCG or RPG. But we still play board and card games.

Yet, in the future, we may see digital technology and games influencing the way we play tabletop ones. What's going to happen as **smart homes** become more common? How will the ever-increasing role of **technology** in our daily lives affect our game playing? And what's next in terms of imagination? Where will our brainstorming take us?

ESSENTIAL QUESTION

What kind of **virtual reality game** would you like to design?

LEGACY GAMES

In most video games, as well as in role-playing games, you can progress through many levels until you get to the end of the game. When you log off, the game saves your place. Later, you can pick up right where you left off. **Legacy** games bring this idea to the board game.

In 2011, designer Rob Daviau (1970–) created *Risk Legacy*. Similar to the original game of *Risk*, the legacy version involves players battling for world domination. But *Risk Legacy* changes each time it's played. Players' decisions in the first game affect the game the next time they play it! Those decisions also physically change the game board. Players place stickers and write on the board with permanent markers. They open sealed packets when certain conditions are met, such as the first battle with three missiles or the construction of the last city. The game changes through 15 play sessions.

Pandemic Legacy
credit: Yoppy (CC BY 2.0)

This legacy concept didn't catch on until a few years later. In 2015, with *Pandemic* designer Matt Leacock, Rob Daviau released *Pandemic Legacy: Season 1*. Players progress through levels of the game, changing the board or other components as they go. The game evolves, just as the viruses do! *Pandemic Legacy: Season 2* was released in 2017.

Why might a game that works this way be so much fun? For one thing, it's almost as though players are getting to play a new game every time. This increases the challenge along with the **novelty** of the play. Players don't get bored the 10th or 11th time through.

The **interactivity** of these legacy games is another reason for their popularity.

Notable Legacy Games

› *Android: Netrunner* (2017)

› *Charterstone* (2017)

› *First Martians: Adventures on the Red Planet* (2016)

› *Gloomhaven* (2015)

› *Pandemic Legacy: Season 1* (2015)

› *Pandemic Legacy: Season 2* (2017)

› *Risk Legacy* (2011)

› *SeaFall* (2016)

› *Ultimate Werewolf Legacy* (2018)

Not only is the game changing and challenging you to make decisions, but the players are changing the game! This dynamic creativity is a pleasure for players to experience.

Following *Pandemic Legacy*'s success, several other legacy games were released, including *Gloomhaven*. It's been described as *Dungeons & Dragons* in a box—a really big, 20-pound box.

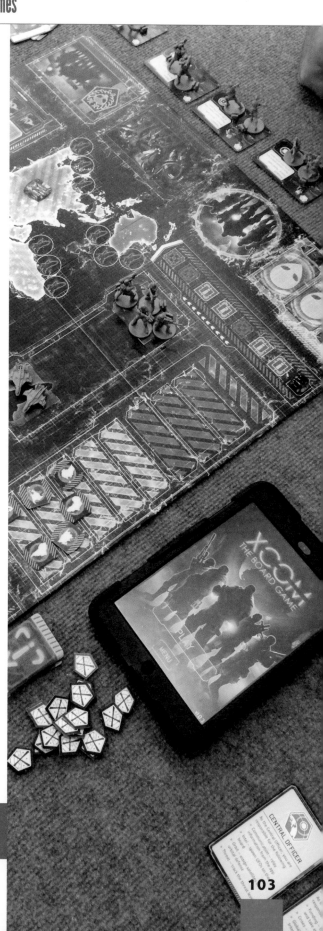

Gloomhaven is a series of *Dungeons & Dragons*-like campaigns that players work through. The game itself acts as the dungeon master. As with other legacy games, as you play *Gloomhaven*, you make choices and change the game. Each dungeon takes about two to three hours to play, with the whole box taking 150 hours to complete.

DIGITAL INTEGRATION

In 2015, *XCOM: The Board Game* was one of the first to use a digital app. As players work together to repel alien invaders, the app coordinates the aliens' plans to enslave the planet. The app is necessary to play the game.

Today, a handful of board games use a digital app as part of game play.

More often, games include optional apps. The *One Night* series of games, for example, includes an app to help time players and lead them through each round. Other games use apps to keep track of certain cards or hit points or to make the setup easier.

Using an app with a board game
credit: Celeste Lindell (CC BY 2.0)

WORDS TO KNOW

3-D printer: a machine that makes a physical object from a three-dimensional model by laying down many thin layers of a material.

three-dimensional (3-D): something that appears solid and can be measured in three directions, length, width, and depth.

SMART GAME TABLES

What if you could make the game table smart? A few companies are proposing to build smart game tables. For example, PlayTable, which is still in development, is a 24-inch touchscreen table that acts as a digital game board. It can interact with physical game pieces, cards, and even smartphones. Players can play face-to-face as well as against others around the world.

Avid gamers, particularly of *Dungeons & Dragons* and other games that use maps, have already built DIY smart tables. These are typically made of a large, flat-screen TV embedded in a large wooden gaming table. The screen displays maps or other graphics from an attached laptop or tablet.

What sorts of possibilities do smart game tables open up for players? What kinds of games might they be able to play that they can't play now?

Gen Con

Gen Con is the biggest and longest-running tabletop game convention in North America. The show includes board, card, roleplaying, and war games as well as video games and science fiction and fantasy authors. Gen Con was founded in 1968 by Gary Gygax, one of the creators of *Dungeons & Dragons*. Gen Con gets its name from its original location, Lake Geneva, Wisconsin. In 2018, more than 60,000 people attended Gen Con, which was held in Indianapolis, Indiana.

3-D-PRINTED GAMES

Instead of buying a game at a store, what if you could download and print the board game and its pieces at home? A **3-D printer** can use plastic and other materials to create **three-dimensional (3-D)** objects, such as game pieces. As 3-D printers become more affordable, hobbyists have already started making their own games and components.

On sites such as MyMiniFactory, people design and share their 3-D designs for game pieces as well as many other objects. Game pieces range from miniatures for wargaming to fantasy chess pieces to goblins for *Dungeons & Dragons* to themed *Settlers of Catan* pieces.

You can see how a game maker used a 3-D printer to enhance his *Dungeons & Dragons* game in this article and video.

PS What else might you be able to do with a 3-D printer?

🔍 Spark Fun 3-D D&D

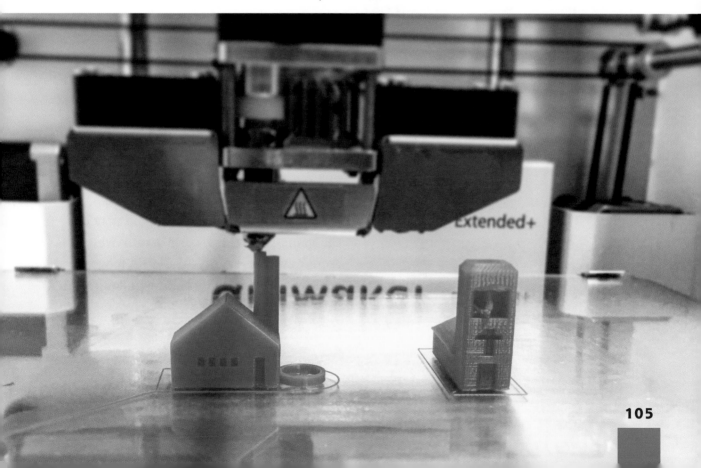

A 3-D printer at work

WORDS TO KNOW

augmented reality (AR): a game that inserts real-world images into the game environment or interacts with real-world objects.

holograph: a special kind of picture that is produced by a laser and looks three-dimensional.

startup company: of or relating to the starting of a new business or company.

AUGMENTED-REALITY GAMES

Augmented Reality (AR) is an interactive experience that blends the real and digital worlds. *Pokémon GO* is one of the best-known AR mobile games. Players use the app on their smartphones to battle monsters at real locations. The real world and virtual worlds blend together as you travel to different places, look at your device, and manipulate the app to interact with the characters.

credit: A1C Christopher R. Morales

AR goggles or helmets let you play even more games. Imagine being able to play a board game using AR technology! Recently, an iOS game called *Star Wars: Jedi Challenges* was introduced, which does just this. It lets you play **holographic** chess just as it's played in the *Star Wars* universe. Using either an iPhone with an AR kit or an AR headset, the game is projected in front of the player!

AR might be a natural next step for some tabletop games. An AR version of *Clue*, for example, might appear in front of you on a tabletop just like a cardboard version. But you could play the game with friends and family who are far away. Distance would no longer keep you from playing with people in other parts of the world, just as you can with online video games.

This kind of display might not be too far in the future!

So far, a few **startup companies** and Kickstarter campaigns are working on this type of AR game. One of those is *Hologrid: Monster Battles* by Tippet Studios. An animator for Industrial Light and Magic as well as for his own studio, Phil Tippet (1951–) designed the 3-D animated aliens for the real *Star Wars* holochess scene! Inspired by that scene, *Hologrid* combines a collectible card game, tactical strategy, and AR. Players collect monster cards and fight them on the holochess-like board.

escape room: a physical adventure game in which players solve puzzles and figure out clues in order to escape a room.

adventure game: a video game in which players participate in an interactive story driven by exploration and puzzle-solving.

Escape Room Board Games

In the last few years, **escape rooms** have become popular. An escape room is a physical **adventure game**. Players have to solve a mystery or a series of puzzles in order to get out of an actual room. Usually, you visit the escape room with a group of friends, for a fee of about $20 to $40 each. Then, you spend a fun hour solving the puzzles together. Now, several game companies are making escape board and card games! These let you set up your own escape room at home. As with physical escape rooms, these board games usually have a theme. For instance, when playing *Escape Room in a Box*, you solve hidden clues in a mad scientist's lair to prevent him from turning everyone into werewolves!

In general, most new tabletop games don't rely heavily on digital technology at this time—and perhaps they won't in the future, either. After all, tabletop games are thrilling to play just as they are today. And the future of the industry is brighter than ever. Sales of tabletop games keep rising. Every year, more than 60,000 people flock to Gen Con, and twice that many gather at Spiel in Essen, Germany, to check out new games! We are in a golden age of board games.

This golden age may in part be due to technology—but not in the way you might think. Board and card games might be booming because we need a break from technology! Video and mobile games are fun. But many of us stare at screens all day. We're playing games, watching TV or videos, looking at social media, doing homework, and so on.

Humans are social creatures. We need to spend time face-to-face. Playing a new board game makes that interaction fresh and positive. What do you think?

ESSENTIAL QUESTION

What kind of virtual reality game would you like to design?

DESIGN A LEGACY GAME

A legacy board game changes through time. The outcome of each game changes the starting point of the next game. For instance, in *Risk Legacy*, a player might conquer Asia the first time playing the game. The next time, they start the game with Asia already under their control. Some legacy games let the players change or mark the board and other game components. In this activity, you're going to make your own version of a legacy game.

▶ **Pick a classic game you might have around the house.** Classic games include checkers, *Scrabble*, or *Monopoly*.

▶ **Think about how you might make the game into a legacy one.** For instance, in legacy *Monopoly*, would you start each game with the properties you bought during the last game? Jot down your ideas in your design notebook.

▶ **Write a paragraph describing how your legacy game would work.** Does the goal of the game change? How do you win? How do the other elements, such as the rules, change?

▶ **Playtest your idea!**

DID YOU KNOW?

Every box of *Risk Legacy* is sealed with a sticker that says: "What's done can never be undone."

Try This!

Make a legacy version of the game you designed in the last chapter!

DESIGN YOUR OWN APP

Several board games today include an app that plays some part in the game. The app might simply help you keep track of scoring or time the rounds, or the app might play an essential role in the game. Think about how you might use an app in one of your favorite games.

❯ **Do a little research on games that have companion apps.** With permission, search online for examples. This article is a good starting place. What cool things can these apps do?

🔍 app enhanced board games

❯ **Pick one of your favorite board, card, or role-playing games.** It should be one that doesn't already have an app.

❯ **Think about how you might add an app to the game.** For instance, does *Settlers of Catan* need a Robber app? Could you add a narrator app to your favorite RPG?

❯ **Draw a diagram or write a paragraph showing how your companion app would work.**

Try This!

Design an app for the game you designed in the last chapter!

Edible Games

Game designer Jenn Sandercock has been developing her own line of edible games. She's putting them in a cookbook called the *Edible Games Cookbook: Play With Your Food.*

🔍 ediblegames

(PS) **You can watch a fun trailer for one of the games,** ***The Order of the Oven Mitt.***

🔍 Order of the Oven Mitt

DESIGN YOUR OWN DIGITAL GAME TABLE

A few serious tabletop gamers have designed their own digital game tables. Some players have sunk a big, flat-screen TV into a table. Others, such as the designers behind PlayTable, imagine a truly digital experience. What type of digital game table would you make?

❯ **Do a little research on digital game tables.** With permission, search online for examples. These are good starting places. What cool things can these tables do?

 ◯ PlayTable

 ◯ DIY gaming table

❯ **Think about what you'd love a game table to be able to do.** Jot these ideas down in your design notebook.

❯ **Draw a diagram or write a paragraph showing how your game table would work.**

Try This!

Design an ad to sell your new digital game table!

Choose-Your-Own-Adventure-Style Games

Remember the *Choose Your Own Adventure* books? In these, the reader gets to pick what the hero does at key points in the book. Every time you read the story, it can come out differently. A game called the *7th Continent* bills itself as one of those books in the form of a board game. Players progress through the story and pull out cards at key moments to determine what happens next. In 2018, the official *Choose Your Own Adventure: House of Danger* game debuted.

SPOT THE TRENDS

Every year, game designers exhibit new games at big trade shows such as Spiel and Gen Con. Hundreds of new games are also posted on Kickstarter in search of funding. In this activity, you're going to research new games!

❯ **With permission, research the new games exhibited at the major trade shows and on Kickstarter.** Start with these. Often, online magazines will do "best of" articles each year following the shows.

- Gen Con
- Spiel
- Kickstarter

❯ **What are some of the hot new games of the year?** Jot those down in your design notebook. Which ones sound like fun? Why?

❯ **Did you spot any new trends?** Is there a certain kind of game that's really popular this year? Jot those down.

❯ **Do these new trends or games give you any ideas for games of your own?** Definitely jot those down!

3-D Printing

One possible future trend might be 3-D printing your own games. A 3-D printer deposits layers of plastic or another material to make a 3-D object—such as a game piece. With permission, do a little research on 3-D printing. How does it work? Think about what kind of game and/or game pieces you could design to print in 3-D. Sketch your ideas in your design notebook. You can try making your 3-D game component using clay or playdough!

Try This!

Based on your research, what's the trend or hot new game going to be next year?

3-D printer: a machine that makes a physical object from a three-dimensional model by laying down many thin layers of a material.

adventure game: a video game in which players participate in an interactive story driven by exploration and puzzle-solving.

agent: a player of a game. This can be a person, a computer, or the game itself.

Alzheimer's disease: a form of dementia that grows worse through time and affects memory, thinking, and behavior.

American dream: an American ideal that says material prosperity means success.

anagram: a word or phrase made by changing the order of the letters in another word or phrase.

archaeologist: a scientist who studies ancient peoples through their bones, tools, and other artifacts.

archaeology: the study of ancient people through the objects they left behind.

aristocrat: a member of a ruling or wealthy class of people.

artifact: an object made by people from past cultures, including tools, pottery, and jewelry.

artificial intelligence (AI): the intelligence of a computer, program, or machine.

augmented reality (AR): a game that inserts real-world images into the game environment or interacts with real-world objects.

avid: eager and enthusiastic.

Aztecs: a Native American people who established an empire in central Mexico between 1300 to the 1500s.

banish: to send someone away from a country or place as an official punishment.

BCE: put after a date, BCE stands for Before Common Era and counts down to zero. CE stands for Common Era and counts up from zero. These nonreligious terms correspond to BC and AD. This book was printed in 2019 CE.

brainstorm: to think creatively and without judgment, often in a group of people.

brick-and-mortar: a term that means a physical store.

calligraphy: the art of beautiful writing.

caudate nucleus: a structure in the brain that plays roles in different types of learning.

chariot: a small cart with two wheels and a platform, pulled by horses.

civilization: a community of people that is advanced in art, science, and government.

collectible card game (CCG): a type of strategy card game with specially designed cards that the player can collect to customize their deck; also called a trading card game.

concept: an idea.

connoisseur: an expert judge in matters of taste.

consumer: a person who buys goods and services.

cooperative: a game that requires players to work together.

critique: a judgment that expresses an opinion about something.

crowdfunding: a way of raising money for a project that involves many people each contributing a small amount.

Crusader: a European soldier who took part in one of the wars fought in the Middle East during the eleventh through thirteenth centuries.

curator: a person who collects and organizes items in a museum.

data: information, facts, and numbers from tests and experiments.

debut: to introduce.

deck building: a game mechanic where the player selects cards to build a custom set of cards.

deduction: using logic or reason to figure out or form an opinion about something.

dementia: a group of brain diseases that cause the gradual decline in a person's ability to think and remember.

descendent: a person related to someone who lived in the past.

digital: involving the use of computer technology.

distribution: the way a product is divided up or shipped out to stores.

distributor: a company that buys a product from a manufacturer and sells and delivers it to a store.

dopamine: a neurotransmitter that produces feelings of pleasure.

drought: a long period of little or no rain.

Ebola: a virus that causes a rare and deadly disease.

ebony: a hard, heavy wood.

economic: having to do with the resources and wealth of a country.

electrode: a conductor through which electricity enters or leaves an object, substance, or region.

endorphins: a group of hormones released in the brain that reduce feelings of pain and improve mood.

epidemic: a disease that hits large groups at the same time and spreads quickly.

escape room: a physical adventure game in which players solve puzzles and figure out clues in order to escape a room.

Eurogame: the term for board games designed in Europe, primarily in Germany.

flow: to move in a steady, smooth way; a state of mind where we feel and perform our best.

foretold: predicted.

freelance: a person who hires out his services independently without working under the control of one boss.

Great Depression: a severe economic downturn during the late 1920s and 1930s that spread around the world.

GLOSSARY

Hindu: a follower of Hinduism, a group of religious beliefs, traditions, and practices from South Asia.

hobby game: a specialty game played by people who are passionate about it.

holograph: a special kind of picture that is produced by a laser and looks three-dimensional.

independently: on one's own or without help.

inequality: differences in opportunity and treatment based on social, ethnic, racial, or economic qualities.

infantry: soldiers trained to fight on foot.

inherent: part of the basic nature of something.

interactive: having a two-way flow of information.

intuitive: having the ability to know or understand things without proof.

investor: a person who gives a company money in exchange for future profits.

iterative process: the process of arriving at a result through repeated rounds in which the product or idea is made a bit better in each round.

lapis lazuli: a deep-blue stone.

Latin: the language of ancient Rome and its empire.

legacy: something that happened or comes from someone in the past.

legion: a large group of soldiers in ancient Rome.

license: to sell the right to publish to a publisher. The author typically gets royalties, or a percentage of the profits, from sales.

logic: the principle, based on math, that things should work together in an orderly way.

makeshift: a temporary substitute or device.

manufacturing: making large quantities of products in factories using machines.

marketing: communicating in different ways to make a business known.

mass market: products that are sold on a large scale.

mechanic: a specific element or type of game play.

merchant: someone who buys and sells goods.

metagame: all the elements of a game the player can participate in.

morality: the distinction between right and wrong or good and bad behavior.

morals: a person's standards of behavior or beliefs.

neuroscientist: someone who studies the development and function of the nervous system, which includes the brain, spinal cord, and nerve cells throughout the body.

neurotransmitter: a brain chemical that carries information throughout the brain and body.

novelty: something that is new or unusual, also something that's popular for a short period of time.

nucleus accumbens (NAc): a region of the brain relating to addiction.

oblong: a stretched-out rectangle with round corners.

oxytocin: a chemical released by your body that makes you happy when you interact with people you like.

packaging: the wrapper and all the parts of a container that holds a product.

pandemic: the outbreak of disease when it spreads across more than once continent. Also the name of a game invented by Matt Leacock.

papyrus: paper made from the papyrus plant, used by the ancient Egyptians.

patent: a government license that gives an inventor or creator the sole right to make and sell a product or invention.

payoff: a good result gained from doing something.

pharaoh: a ruler of ancient Egypt.

playtest: the process of testing a new game for bugs and design flaws before bringing it to market.

plaything: a form of entertainment that people interact and play with. It can be a toy, game, or puzzle.

posh: expensive, upper class.

prestigious: something inspiring respect and admiration.

principle: an important idea or belief that guides an individual or community.

product engineer: a person who designs and develops something that will be sold.

promote: to make people aware of something, such as a new product, through advertising, or to make something more popular or well known.

prototype: an early version of a design used for testing.

psychologist: a person who studies the mind and behavior.

pyramid of needs: a way to organize human needs into most-important and less-important categories.

raja: a king or prince in India.

rampage: uncontrolled and usually violent behavior.

reform: a change to improve something.

resource: something that people can use.

rosette: a design shaped like a rose.

royalty: money paid to the creator of something for every unit sold.

sanction: to approve.

Sanskrit: the primary language of Hinduism.

serotonin: a neurotransmitter with a wide variety of functions in the body. It contributes to feelings of well-being and happiness.

settlement: a place where a group of people moves to start a new community.

severe acute respiratory syndrome (SARS): a contagious and sometimes fatal respiratory illness that causes flu-like symptoms.

simultaneous: at the same time.

smart home: a house in which all electric devices are monitored or controlled by a computer.

solidify: to make something more solid or stronger.

species: a group of living things that are closely related and can produce young.

spiritual: relating to the mind and spirit instead of the physical world.

staple: something that is used often.

startup company: of or relating to the starting of a new business or company.

strategy: a careful plan for achieving a goal. Also, the skill of making and carrying out those plans.

suit: all the cards that have the same symbol, such as hearts or spades, in a deck.

tactics: a carefully planned action or strategy to achieve something.

tarot cards: special cards used to tell fortunes.

technology: the tools, methods, and systems used to solve a problem or do work.

theme: a central, recurring idea or concept.

three-dimensional (3-D): something that appears solid and can be measured in three directions, length, width, and depth.

trump: a playing card or suit that's chosen above others to win a trick when a card of a different suit is played.

user experience: the experience of a person using a product.

ventral tegmental area (VTA): a group of nerve cells in the midbrain responsible for releasing dopamine.

vice: a bad behavior or habit.

Vikings: a group of seafaring pirates and traders from Scandinavia who migrated throughout Europe between the eighth and eleventh centuries.

virtual reality game: a game designed for a wearable screen that makes players feel as though they are inside the game itself.

virtue: any good quality or trait.

virus: an extremely small particle that causes disease and is spread from person to person.

war game: a game based on military experiences.

wholesale: large quantities of an item bought at a cheaper price in order to resell at a higher price.

Metric Conversions

Use this chart to find the metric equivalents to the English measurements in this book. If you need to know a half measurement, divide by two. If you need to know twice the measurement, multiply by two. How do you find a quarter measurement? How do you find three times the measurement?

English	Metric
1 inch	2.5 centimeters
1 foot	30.5 centimeters
1 yard	0.9 meter
1 mile	1.6 kilometers
1 pound	0.5 kilogram
1 teaspoon	5 milliliters
1 tablespoon	15 milliliters
1 cup	237 milliliters

BOOKS

Donovan, Tristan. *It's All a Game: The History of Board Games from Monopoly to Settlers of Catan.* Thomas Dunne Books, 2017.

Tinsman, Brian. *The Game Inventor's Guidebook: How to Invent and Sell Board Games, Card Games, Role-Playing Games, & Everything in Between!* Morgan James Publishing, 2008.

MAGAZINES

Casual Game Insider
casualgamerevolution.com/magazine

Tabletop Gaming
tabletopgaming.co.uk

Meoples
meoplesmagazine.com

You can find a longer list here!
boardgamegeek.com/wiki/page/Game_Magazines

WEBSITES

Crash Course Games
youtube.com/watch?v=QPqR2wOs8WI&list=
PL8dPuuaLjXtPTrc_yg73RghJEOdobAplG

Board Game Geek
boardgamegeek.com

TableTop on Geek & Sundry
geekandsundry.com/shows/tabletop

How to Play on Geek & Sundry
geekandsundry.com/shows/how-to-play

Spellslingers (Magic: The Gathering show)
geekandsundry.com/shows/spellslingers

Dungeons & Dragons
dnd.wizards.com

Magic: The Gathering
magic.wizards.com/en

How to Design a Tabletop Game – Stonemaier Games
stonemaiergames.com/kickstarter/how-to-design-a-tabletop-game

Board Game Design Lab
boardgamedesignlab.com

The Game Crafter
thegamecrafter.com

Matt Leacock Games
leacock.com/blog/2017/5/18/game-design-resources

RESOURCES

QR CODE GLOSSARY

ESSENTIAL QUESTIONS

Introduction: What is your favorite game to play? Why?

Chapter 1: Have games changed since we started playing them thousands of years ago?

Chapter 2: Why do people invent new games?

Chapter 3: What are some reasons humans play games?

Chapter 4: Where do ideas for games come from?

Chapter 5: Why are game design and game development considered different parts of the game-making process?

Chapter 6: What kind of virtual reality game would you like to design?